Big Book of
Christmas
Crafts™

Edited by Laura Scott

HOUSE of
WHITE
BIRCHES

PUBLISHERS
SINCE 1947

Big Book of Christmas Crafts

Editor: Laura Scott
Associate Editor: Cathy Reef
Design Associate: Vicki Blizzard
Editorial Assistant: Katie Furtaw
Technical Editor: Läna Schurb
Book and Cover Design: Jessi Butler
Copy Editor: Michelle Beck, Mary Martin
Publications Coordinators: June Sprunger, Tanya Turner

Photography: Tammy Christian, Jeff Chilcote, Justin P. Wiard, Kelly Heydinger, Nancy Sharp
Photography Assistant: Linda Quinlan

Production Coordinator: Brenda Gallmeyer
Graphic Arts Supervisor: Ronda Bechinski
Graphic Artist: Edith Teegarden
Production Assistants: Janet Bowers, Marj Morgan
Traffic Coordinator: Sandra Beres
Technical Artists: Liz Morgan, Mitchell Moss, Travis Spangler, Chad Summers

Publishers: Carl H. Muselman, Arthur K. Muselman
Chief Executive Officer: John Robinson
Publishing Marketing Director: David McKee
Book Marketing Manager: Craig Scott
Product Development Director: Vivian Rothe
Publishing Services Manager: Brenda R. Wendling

Printed in the United States of America
First Printing: 2002
Library of Congress Number: 2001089862
ISBN: 1-882138-85-6

Special thanks to Swiss Village Retirement Community, Berne, Ind., for the photo locations.
Olga Tinker, pages 7 and 9, from Charmaine Model Agency, Fort Wayne, Ind.

A Note From the Editor!

Every crafter I know looks forward to the holidays with the greatest of anticipation! Gathering family, friends and other loved ones, the holidays bring people together in a way that is special and unique. If you're a crafter like me, then you love to make gifts and goodies for all those wonderful people you love and cherish!

One of my favorite winter activities is to invite my crafting friends to my house for a party. Each friend brings several projects she's working on plus lots of crafting supplies. We sit around the kitchen table and in the living room and craft to our hearts' content! It's a great way to spend time together while making goodies for the winter festivities! Last year, we invited a noncrafter. By the evening's end, she was bustling with excitement and had crafted three simply delightful gifts!

In this colorful and festive book, you'll find dozens upon dozens upon dozens of creative ideas for making the Christmas season bright, cheery and very crafty! From one-of-a-kind gifts that are economical yet lovely to gorgeous home accents to make your house into that perfect holiday home, you'll find just what you want to make this season extra-special! Because so many crafters enjoy working in a variety of media, we've strived to bring you an inviting selection of projects worked in a wide variety of techniques! Painting, wood crafts, clay crafts, sewing, felt crafts, wearables and many more await you!

We've called this book *Big Book of Christmas Crafts* because we've packed every page with extra value and Christmas cheer. You won't find any other book on the market that has as many projects with as many bright and colorful photos and easy-to-follow instructions. With each book, we at House of White Birches want to bring you more value, more creativity and more crafting fun!

I hope you love crafting from this book as much as my staff and I loved putting it together—just for you!

Warm regards,

Laura Scott

Contents

Christmas Home Decor

Gifts and Goodies

Tree Trims & Ornaments

Holiday Hospitality

Festive Fashions

Gifts & Goodies

Delight each and every friend and loved one on your gift list with one-of-a-kind handcrafted gifts! Not only will you save time and money, but your personal gifts are also sure to be treasured throughout the year!

Beaded Elegance

Sew gold beads and ribbon onto a luscious piece of red velveteen
for an elegant stocking to hang from the chimney!

Design by Chris Malone

Materials

- Velveteen fabrics: ½ yard red, 6½" x 11½" black
- ½ yard red lining fabric
- Wire-edge ribbons: 2 yards ⅜"-wide metallic gold, 1 yard ⅞"-wide red with gold edge, ⅓ yard 1½"-wide green with gold edge, 1 yard ⅜"-wide metallic gold
- Approximately 75 size 6/0 gold glass beads
- 27 (½") gold bugle beads
- 1½" brass heart charm
- 1⅓ yards ⅛"-wide gold braid trim
- Beading thread
- Metallic gold embroidery floss
- Tissue paper
- Fabric adhesive*
- Seam sealant
- Needles: embroidery needle, beading needle
- Matching sewing threads
- Sewing machine (optional)

Fabri-Tac adhesive from Beacon.

Project Notes

Refer to photo, patterns and Figs. 1–5 throughout.

Before cutting fabric, use a photocopier with enlarging capabilities to enlarge stocking pattern 185 percent.

Use ¼" seam allowance throughout.

Instructions

1. Cut two stockings, reversing one, from red velveteen and two, reversing one, from lining fabric. If desired, overcast edges of velveteen with wide zigzag stitch to prevent fraying.

2. *Mark positions of ribbon rosettes:* Place a pin 4" down and 3" in from left edge of stocking. Measure down at an angle 2½" and place another pin. Continue until there are nine pins about 2½" apart going down stocking and into foot.

3. *Ribbon rosettes:* Cut ⅜" wired gold ribbon into nine 8" pieces. Knot one end of one piece; at opposite end, gently pull wire from one edge to gather (Fig. 1). Continue pulling until entire side is completely gathered; do not cut off wire end. To form rose, hold knotted end in one hand and begin to spiral-wrap gathered ribbon around it with other hand. To end, fold raw edge in and secure rose by wrapping wire tightly around knotted base; cut off excess (Fig. 2). Shape petals. Repeat to make a total of nine rosettes.

Fig. 1

4. Using beading thread and beading needle, sew a gold glass bead in center of ribbon rosette and then sew rosette to pin location. Using same thread, sew three bugle beads radiating out from base of rosette along one side and four more gold glass beads clustered around edge of rosette on other side. Repeat with remaining rosettes.

Fig. 2

5. Sew remaining gold glass beads randomly between rosettes, avoiding seam areas.

6. Pin stocking front and back together, right sides facing. Sew around stocking, leaving it open at top. Clip curves; turn right side out.

7. *Cuff:* Trace "JOY" onto tissue paper; pin to black velveteen so top of "J" is 1" from top and 4½" from left edge. Using 4 strands metallic gold embroidery floss, backstitch letters onto velveteen through tissue. Carefully tear tissue away when stitching is complete. Add a French knot at tip of each letter.

"Joy"

8. Sew short ends of cuff together, right sides facing. Turn right side out; fold cuff in half lengthwise so tube is 3½" tall. Slip cuff inside top of stocking with embroidery against wrong side of stocking front and cuff seam at center back. Sew cuff to stocking and turn cuff out over top of stocking.

9. *Lining:* Pin lining front and back together right sides facing and sew together, leaving top open. Clip curves but do not turn right side out. Turn and press ¼" hem at top. Slip lining inside stocking; match side seams. Slipstitch top of lining to top of stocking and cuff seams.

10. Apply seam sealant to end of gold braid trim. ***Hint:*** *Apply sealant to spot near end of trim. When dry, cut through sealed area to prevent fraying.* Working with about 4" at a time, lift cuff and apply a very thin line of adhesive to seam; press trim over

seam. Continue all around, ending under cuff on other side. Apply seam sealant to end of trim; cut off excess and reserve for hanger.

11. *Ribbon on cuff:* Make four-loop bow from ⅜" gold ribbon. Wrap center of bow with thread; notch ends and set aside. Cut red ribbon into one 6" and three 10" lengths. Knot one end of one 10" piece; at opposite end, gently pull wire from one edge to gather (Fig. 1). Continue pulling until entire side is completely gathered; do not cut off wire end. To form rose, hold knotted end in one hand and begin to spiral-wrap gathered ribbon around it with other hand. To end, fold raw edge in and secure rose by wrapping wire tightly around knotted base; cut off excess wire (Fig. 2). Shape petals with fingers as desired. Repeat to make a total of three rosettes.

12. *Rosebud:* Hold 6" red ribbon horizontally and fold one end down at 90-degree angle. Roll edge of ribbon toward other end twice to make rolled center. Holding base of bud center in one hand, hold working end of ribbon with other hand and fold ribbon back with a half-twist while turning the center toward the working end (Fig. 3). Fold and turn again and fold working end down and wrap ends with thread.

Fig. 3

13. *Leaves:* Cut green ribbon into three 4" lengths. Fold ends of one piece in toward center at 90-degree angles (Fig. 4). Using green thread, sew gathering stitch along bottom edge beside wire (Fig. 5). Pull thread to gather tightly; wrap thread around stitches to secure; knot and clip thread ends. Repeat to make a total of three leaves.

14. Tack or glue embellishment to stocking, placing bow at an angle and tucking leaves around bow. Add roses and rosebuds, covering ends of leaves.

15. Using gold embroidery floss, backstitch a short line extending down from bow and attach charm. Add a drop of glue under top of heart charm if desired.

16. *Hanging loop:* From remaining gold braid, cut 8" piece; seal ends. Knot ends and tack to inside seam of stocking on right side so loop extends over top of stocking. ❊

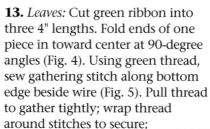

Fig. 4   **Fig. 5**

Stocking
Enlarge 185% before cutting
Cut 2, reversing 1, from red velveteen and 2, reversing 1, from lining fabric

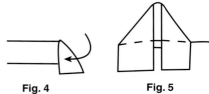

Holly Gift Box

This holly-covered box makes a glittery container for a small gift or a festive home accent.
Use a different paper napkin to change the look to match your other holiday decorations.

Design by Joan Fee

Materials

- Appliqué glue*
- Paper dinner napkins with holly print or other desired design
- Tree-shaped papier-mâché box with lid
- Iridescent glitter
- Foam paintbrush
- Shallow tray or box lid

Aleene's Paper Napkin Appliqué Glue from Duncan.

Instructions

1. Remove printed ply from napkins; discard unprinted plies.

2. Trim excess from one napkin, leaving a large enough piece to cover lid's top and sides; trim a second, leaving it large enough to cover sides of box.

3. Brush top and sides of lid with napkin glue. Center napkin over top and smooth it over glued surfaces with your fingers.

4. Brush sides of box with glue. Position napkin along glued surfaces, easing the excess and trimming it off as you go. Using same technique, cover bottom of box. ***Note:*** *If some areas are not covered with napkin, brush the bare areas with a little glue and place a "patch" cut from the napkin over the glue.*

5. Place pieces on tray or in box lid; brush surfaces with glue and immediately sprinkle with iridescent glitter. Shake off excess glitter and hang box and lid to dry completely.* ❈

Winter Glow Candles

These festive candles will add a warm Christmas feeling to any centerpiece.
Surround each with evergreen or stand them alone.

Designs by Vicki Schreiner

Materials
Both Candles

- 2 (3" x 6") red pillar candles
- Candle and soap painting medium*
- Acrylic paints*: mocha brown, tompte red, brown velvet, empire gold, Bridgeport grey, white, black, dark foliage green, eucalyptus
- Paintbrushes: ½" glaze/wash, #4 shader, #4 round, #0 liner
- Tissue paper
- Black graphite paper
- Dull No. 2 pencil
- Removable adhesive tape
- Toothpick
- Textured paper towel

Ceramcoat Candle & Soap Painting Medium #07014 and acrylic paints from Delta.

Project Notes

Before transferring pattern, use photocopier with enlarging capabilities to enlarge patterns 125 percent.

To transfer patterns, refer to instructions for "Using Transfer & Graphite Paper" in the General Instructions, page 190. Do not transfer stippling dots; these are for your reference when shading.

For all painting steps, mix each color of paint with an equal amount of candle and soap painting medium.

Refer to instructions for base-coating under "Painting Techniques" in the General Instructions on page 190, but apply three or four coats of paint, allowing paint to dry between coats.

Shading: Work on small areas at a time. Load #4 round brush with a small amount of paint, then stroke on palette to remove most of color. Referring to stippled areas on original pattern, apply paint to area to be shaded. Quickly stroke the brush across a paper towel and then pat the dry brush onto applied paint to soften and blend it. *Patting is the key to success.* Allow to dry, then repeat as needed to darken it.

Lining: Pull #0 liner brush through pool of paint, twirling as you go until bristles form a point. Use flowing strokes, making sure bristles are vertical and not on their sides. Use just the tip of the bristles as you would a pencil.

Preparation

1. Lightly buff surface of candle with a textured paper towel.

2. Transfer main design using No. 2 pencil and light pressure. Do not transfer stippling dots.

3. Using ½" glaze/wash brush, apply a coat of candle and soap painting medium to entire surface of candle, painting over transferred design. Let dry.

Painting

1. Base-coat designs: *ribbons and bows*—gold; *all leaves*—eucalyptus; *flowers*—white; *berries*—base-coat first with white, then let dry; apply a single coat of red; let dry and apply additional red at centers. Let base-coating dry completely.

2. Lightly transfer details to dry base-coated design.

3. Add shading, allowing paints to dry between applications: *ribbons and bows*—shade first with mocha brown, then with brown velvet; *all leaves*—dark green; *flowers*—gray.

4. Using same technique as for shading, highlight tips of all leaves with white.

5. Add lining: *ribbons and bows*—dark green and red; *veins in holly leaves and stems*—dark green; *pine boughs*—line first with dark green;

let dry, then line tip of each needle with white.

6. Add details:

Christmas Flowers: Randomly apply several tiny dots of red and mocha brown to center of each flower; let dry. Apply three larger dots of gold to center of each flower.

Holiday Holly: Using liner and

white paint, apply small comma-stroke highlight to right side of each berry. Dot top of each berry with black; let dry. Dot each black dot with a tiny dot of white.

7. Using ½" glaze/wash brush, apply one coat of candle and soap painting medium to all sides of candles; let dry. ❊

Christmas Flowers
Enlarge 125% before transferring

Holiday Holly
Enlarge 125% before transferring

Gift Totes

Children and grown-ups alike will love receiving these whimsical gift bags!
Let your favorite little girl use one as a purse to carry around.

Design by Mary Ayres

Materials

- Set of 3 wooden boxes with handles, 5", 5½" and 6"*
- 1 yard ⅜"-wide wire-edge silver ribbon
- Silly shapes rubber stamps*
- Acrylic paints*: lavender, bright green, true red
- Shimmering silver metallic acrylic paint*
- #8 natural bristle brush
- Glaze applicator or 2" square household sponge
- Glue*
- Paper plate

Wooden boxes from Provo Craft; Simply Stamps Silly Shapes #53863 rubber stamps from Plaid; Americana acrylic paints and Dazzling Metallics paint from DecoArt; Stamp Decor glaze applicator from Plaid; and Kids Choice Glue for Beacon.

Project Notes

Refer to photo throughout.

Stamping: Pour paint onto paper plate. Dip one side of applicator or sponge into paint, then dab paint onto stamp, making sure entire stamp surface has paint on it. Press stamp down firmly, then lift straight up so paint does not smear. Wash paint from applicator and stamp as soon as you are finished stamping.

Instructions

1. Paint all surfaces of small box bright green, medium box red and large box lavender; let dry.

2. Using silver paint and a different stamp for each box, stamp designs all over box exteriors, spacing designs evenly and going in all directions. Let dry.

3. Cut ribbon into three equal pieces. Tie each in a bow and glue one to each box. ✤

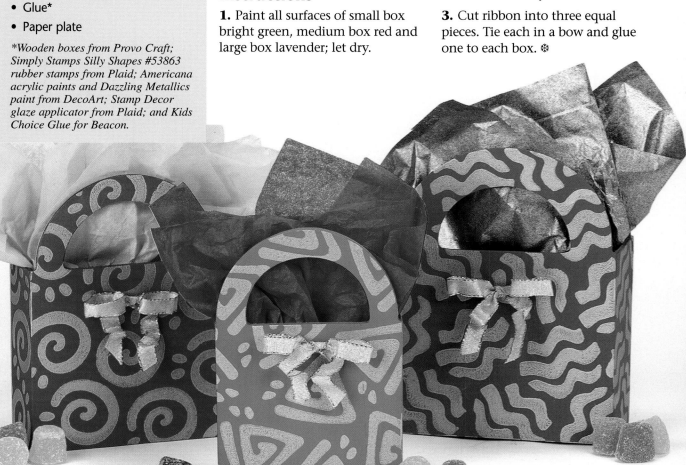

Festive Christmas Soaps

Bring Christmas cheer into your bathroom with these green and red scented soaps.
The chrome basket makes them ready to give away—if you're willing to!

Designs by Charlene Messerle

Materials

- Soap products*: 1 pound glycerin soap base, red and green soap colors, Christmas scent, 8½" x 3" rectangular metal candle/soap mold
- Pyrex glass measuring cup
- Pan
- Wooden spoon
- Acrylic paints*: woodland night green, bright red
- Decorative snow*
- Flat paintbrush
- 5" x 5" x 3" chrome basket with handles
- Red crinkled paper shreds
- Wooden cutouts*: 4 Christmas trees or stockings per soap
- Red and green raffia
- Plastic wrap
- Thick tacky craft glue

Soapsations soap products from Yaley; Ceramcoat acrylic paints and decorative snow from Delta; and Woodsies Christmas cutouts from Forster.

Project Note

Refer to manufacturer's directions throughout when using soap-making products.

Soap

1. Cut glycerin soap base into cubes.

2. Using double-boiler method specified in manufacturer's instructions, melt soap: Place ⅓ of soap base into Pyrex glass measuring cup; place in a pan containing 3"–4" water. Stir with a wooden

Snowflake Gift Tags

Make your gifts extra special with this set of delightful snowflake tags. They also make memorable keepsakes as tree ornaments after the gifts are unwrapped!

Design by Samantha McNesby

Materials

- 2 (2") wooden snowflake cutouts with pre-drilled hole*
- Acrylic paints*: white wash, blue chiffon
- Glorious gold metallic acrylic paint*
- 8" 22-gauge black craft wire
- Wire snips or craft scissors
- Needle-nose pliers
- Foam paintbrush
- Old scruffy paintbrush
- Toothpick
- Fine-point black marker
- 1" x 5" piece holiday-print fabric

Snowflake cutouts from Lara's Crafts; and Americana and Dazzling Metallics acrylic paints from DecoArt.

Project Notes

Refer to photo throughout.

Let all paints and ink dry between applications.

See directions for base-coating and dry-brushing under "Painting Techniques" in General Instructions, page 190.

Instructions

1. Using foam brush, base-coat snowflakes with white paint.

2. Using scruffy paintbrush, dry-brush edges of snowflakes with blue.

3. Using toothpick dipped in gold, add dots to each arm of snowflakes.

4. Using marker, write "To:" and recipient's name on one snowflake, and "From:" and giver's name on the other, making sure pre-drilled holes are at tops of snowflakes.

5. Coil one end of wire with needle-nose pliers or around pencil; thread on snowflakes; coil other end of wire. Fold wire loosely in half with snowflakes together, and twist wire (snowflakes should be below the twist, near the ends). Tie fabric strip around twisted portion of wire. ❈

Festive Christmas Soaps

spoon to melt; do not overheat. *Do not leave melting soap unattended.*

3. Add red coloring and scent to melted soap base; pour into mold and let harden.

4. Repeat steps 2 and 3, substituting green coloring for red.

5. Cut red and green soap into cubes; place in mold.

6. Melt remaining clear glycerin;

add scent and pour over colored cubes. Let harden.

7. Remove soap from mold; cut into ¾"–1" slices. Leave slices whole or cut in half as desired. Wrap each piece in plastic wrap.

Finishing

1. Wrap several strands of red or green raffia around each wrapped slice and tie ends in a bow.

2. Paint wooden tree and stocking cutouts green or red as desired; let dry.

3. Apply decorative snow to cuffs of stockings on one side, applying it so that two stockings face right and two face left.

4. Glue wooden cutouts together in pairs, sandwiching ends of raffia bows in between and varying the positions of the cutouts along the strands.

5. Fill chrome basket with red crinkled paper shreds; nestle soaps in shredded paper. ❈

Santa & Rudolph Gift Bag

Corrugated paper and small embellishments turn a plain paper bag into a festive gift!

Design by Chris Malone

Materials

- 8" x 9¾" red paper bag with handles
- 7½" x 9" kraft brown corrugated paper
- Card stock: 1 sheet each red and brown, small pieces light tan, dark tan, black, green and wavy corrugated white
- 2 (¼") round wooden plugs
- 4 (5mm) black cabochons
- Buttons: ¾" black, ⅞" tan, ⅝" tan, 3 (½") red
- Several strands red raffia
- 18" 24-gauge brown plastic-coated wire
- Acrylic paints: dark rosy flesh, red
- Small paintbrush
- Pink powdered cosmetic blusher
- Cotton-tip swab
- Black fine-line permanent marking pen
- Tacky craft glue

Project Note

Refer to photo and patterns throughout.

Gift Bag

1. Center and glue corrugated rectangle on front of bag.

2. Cut one Santa hat and suit from red card stock, one Santa face from light tan, one hat trim, one suit trim and two sleeve trims from dark tan, boots and four mittens, reversing two, from black, two trees from green, beard and two mustache halves, reversing one, from wavy corrugated white, and one ½" x 3" strip from brown.

3. Arrange Santa suit, face, hat, boots, beard, mustache halves and two mittens on bag front; glue in place. Glue two trees together, inserting ½" of brown strip in bottom for trunk. Lay tree trunk across mitten on right and one end of brown wire on other mitten; top with remaining mittens and glue in place. Glue suit, sleeve and hat trims in place.

4. Paint one plug dark rosy flesh; let dry. Using cotton-tip swab, apply cosmetic blusher to face for cheeks. Glue plug to Santa's face for nose; glue two cabochons to face for eyes.

5. Glue black button to center front of Santa's suit; glue red buttons to tree; glue small tan button to tip of hat.

Rudolph

1. Cut two antlers, reversing one, from light tan card stock; cut two reindeer heads and two ears, reversing one, from brown. Fold 5" x 6½"

piece brown card stock in half to measure 5" x 3¼"; positioning top of reindeer pattern along fold, cut one reindeer from doubled brown card stock.

2. Apply glue to one head; press inner edges of ears and ends of antlers into place. Make a few coils in free end of wire attached to Santa's hand; press wire end into glue on reindeer's head. Top with remaining head and press with fingers to secure.

3. Paint remaining plug red; let dry. Glue plug to reindeer's face for nose; glue two cabochons to face for eyes. Draw straight line down from nose with black marking pen.

4. Glue reindeer head to front upper left corner of body.

Finishing

Tie raffia in bow around handle of bag; trim ends. Glue large tan button to center of bow. ❈

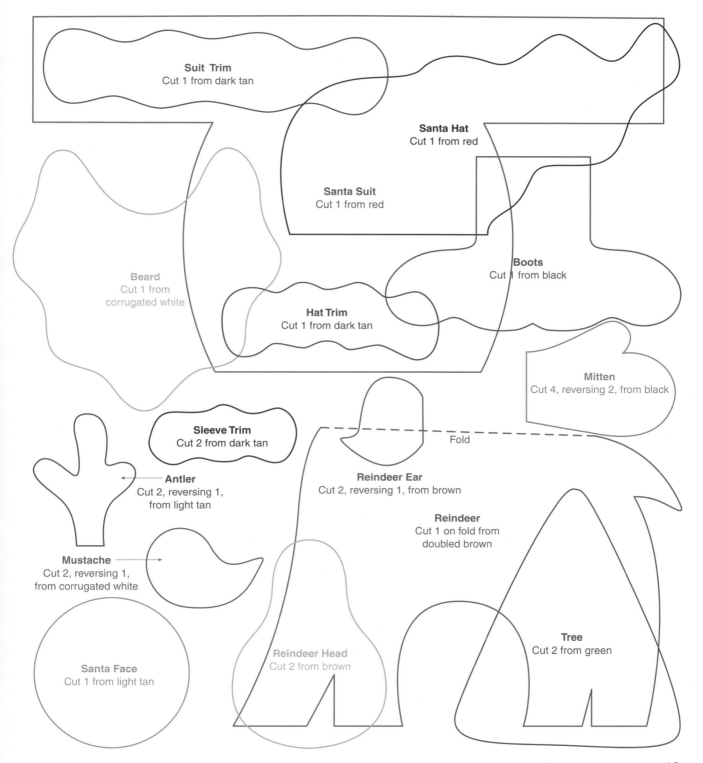

Suit Trim
Cut 1 from dark tan

Santa Hat
Cut 1 from red

Santa Suit
Cut 1 from red

Boots
Cut 1 from black

Beard
Cut 1 from corrugated white

Hat Trim
Cut 1 from dark tan

Mitten
Cut 4, reversing 2, from black

Sleeve Trim
Cut 2 from dark tan

Fold

Antler
Cut 2, reversing 1, from light tan

Reindeer Ear
Cut 2, reversing 1, from brown

Reindeer
Cut 1 on fold from doubled brown

Mustache
Cut 2, reversing 1, from corrugated white

Santa Face
Cut 1 from light tan

Reindeer Head
Cut 2 from brown

Tree
Cut 2 from green

Frosty Gift Bag

Give gifts in these simple and delightful snowman bags all winter long!

Design by Chris Malone

Materials

- Brown paper lunch sack
- Card stock: 2 sheets white, 1 sheet black, small pieces orange and green
- 2½" x 8½" strip red-and-black checked fabric
- Buttons: 2 (½") black, 3 (¾") red
- 24" white twisted paper cord
- 18" 18-gauge white plastic-coated wire
- Dark pink acrylic paint
- 2½" square sponge
- Black fine-line permanent marking pen
- Seam sealant
- Round hole punch
- Tacky craft glue

Project Note

Refer to photo and patterns throughout.

Instructions

1. Measure up 6" from bottom of lunch sack and cut off top; reserve top. Fold bottom of bag up into a W shape so front and back edges are even. Cut paper cord in half and bend each piece into a curve for handles. Carefully glue ends inside corners of bag with one handle on front and one handle on back of sack. Cut four small squares from reserved bag top; apply glue and press over ends of handles to help secure them to bag.

2. Cut two snowman heads from white card stock, two hat crowns and brims from black, two holly leaves from green, one nose from orange and one heart from red.

3. Trim sponge to make a 2½" circle. Dip into dark pink paint and press lightly to one head to make cheeks, positioning cheeks about 1½" up from bottom and ½" in from sides of face. Let dry. ***Note:*** *If paper warps, press under books for a few minutes.*

4. Using marking pen, draw "running stitch" around edges of both heads, holly leaves and nose; add "running stitch" veins down centers of leaves. Draw wiggly line with straight stitches around cheeks.

5. Glue head with cheeks to front and other head to back of sack with bottom edges of heads even with bottom of sack. Glue hat crowns and brims to top of bag and heads

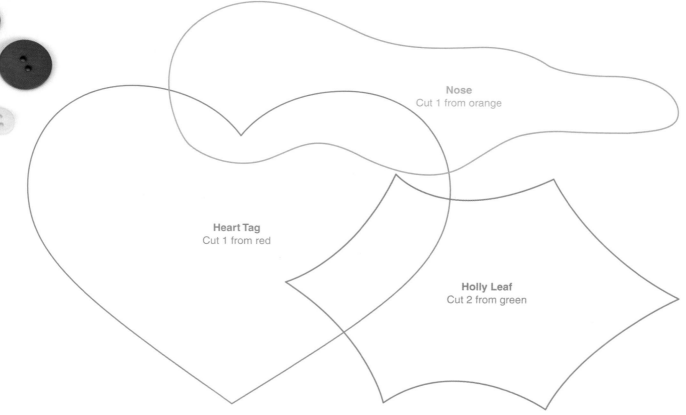

Nose
Cut 1 from orange

Heart Tag
Cut 1 from red

Holly Leaf
Cut 2 from green

at an angle, reversing angle on back of bag so edges match when bag is folded shut.

6. On front of bag, glue nose to face and holly leaves to hat. Glue black buttons to face for eyes and one red button to base of holly leaves.

7. *Bow tie:* Cut 2½" x 7" strip from fabric; apply seam sealant to edges and let dry. Cut 2¼" x 2½" piece; fold long edges ½" to wrong side and wrap around center of strip, overlapping ends and gluing them together to gather center of bow. Apply glue to center back of bow; press onto bottom of face on front of sack.

8. Using hole punch, punch hole in top center of heart. Push one end of wire through hole and curl it a few times around a pencil, then push end through two holes in one red button. Curl wire end again on back of button to hold button in place. Push other end of wire through holes in remaining button. Wrap center of wire around handle, curling wire as desired. ❄

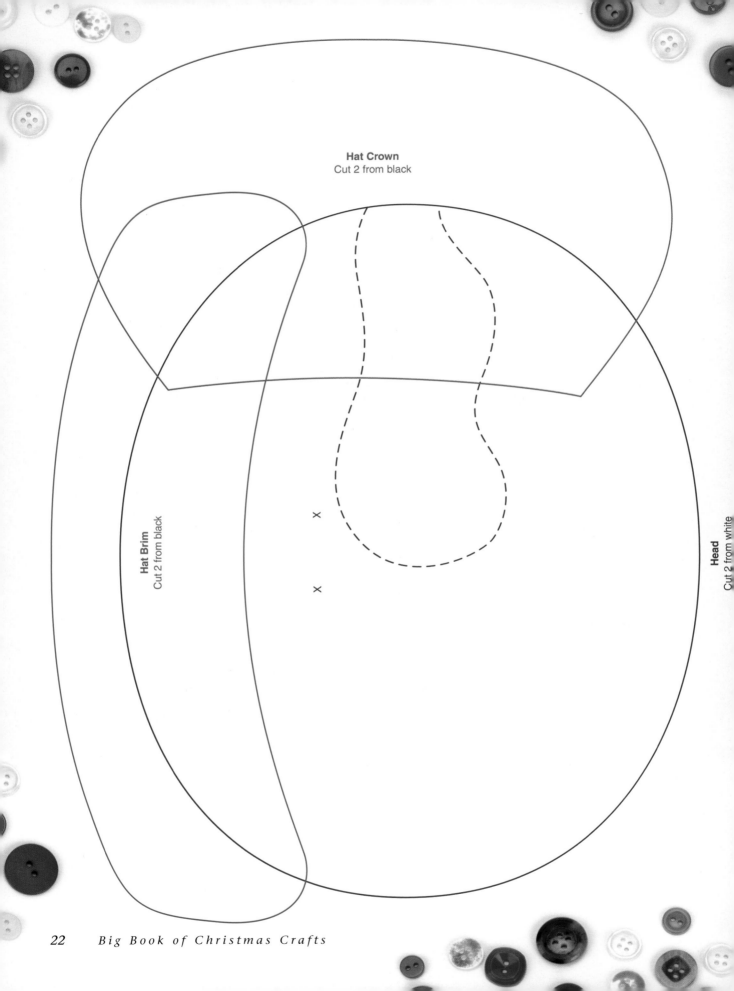

Hat Crown
Cut 2 from black

Hat Brim
Cut 2 from black

Head
Cut 2 from white

Reindeer Photo Holder

Let Rudolph show off your favorite Christmas memory in his antlers.
He's handy for business cards or notes, too!

Design by June Fiechter

Materials

- 2½" terra-cotta flowerpot
- 2½" circle green felt
- Modeling compound*: white, cherry red
- 12" dark green raffia paper*
- ½" silver jingle bell
- 2 (¼") round black cabochons
- 12" fine hemp cord
- Tacky glue*
- Small scruffy paintbrush
- Flocking paints*: baby pink, vanilla cream, dark brown
- Gloss-finish varnish
- 20" ⅜"-wide soft aluminum modeling wire
- Baking sheet
- Waxed paper
- Oven

Fimo Soft modeling compound; Raffia Accents paper and Soft Flock paints from Plaid; Crafter's Pick Ultimate Tacky Glue from API; and Wireform Armature Modeling Wire #50070W from Amaco.

Project Notes

Refer to photo and Fig. 1 throughout.

Refer to manufacturers' instructions for working with modeling compound and flocked paints.

Modeling & Assembly

1. Place waxed paper on baking sheet; preheat oven to 265 degrees.

2. Roll cherry modeling compound into a ¾" ball for nose; place on waxed paper. Roll white modeling compound into two identical teardrop shapes ¾" wide x 1¼" long for ears. Indent inner ears by pressing end and side of paintbrush into

each ear at rounded end. Place ears on waxed paper.

3. Press a lump of modeling compound about the size of a small egg into the bottom of the flowerpot, pressing out all air bubbles.

4. Bend wire into Y-shape as shown in Fig. 1. Note that the finished shape should not be perfectly flat. Rather, the left-hand wire should be slightly in front of the central V, which in turn should be slightly in front of the right-hand piece of wire. Use a 3" x 5" card or business card to check that Y-shape will hold card securely.

5. Poke stem of wire Y-shape through hole in pot into modeling compound; press compound firmly around wires.

6. Press the ears onto top of pot against wires; press red ball onto front of pot just above rim for nose.

7. Place pot on waxed paper and bake as directed. Let cool completely.

Painting & Finishing

1. Apply paints to reindeer one

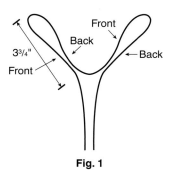

Fig. 1

color at a time in the following order: *vanilla cream:* head and ears; *dark brown:* hair on top of pot (add a curl over edge onto side of pot); *baby pink:* inner ears. Let paints dry.

2. Glue on cabochons for eyes.

3. Open raffia; glue around base of pot. Craft a small bow of raffia and glue on raffia to left of center. Wrap hemp cord around raffia-covered pot rim; thread on jingle bell at bow and knot cord.

4. Using only the adhesive from the baby pink flocked paint, add a highlight oval to the nose. When completely dry, apply varnish to nose only. ❃

Frosty Votives

*These frosty candle holders will add a warm glow to any room during the holidays.
Give them to friends after your Christmas party to brighten up their homes, too.*

Designs by Bill Palasty for Delta Technical Coatings

Materials
All Three Designs
- Holiday stencil minis*: Santa's On His Way, holly wreath
- Self-adhesive holiday stencil: Holy & Peace
- Apparel stencils: Christmas Joy pocket stencil
- Acrylic paints*: golden brown, Christmas green, ocean reef blue, old parchment, medium flesh, bright red, white

- 14K gold paint*
- Stencil spray adhesive*
- ¼" stencil brushes*
- Printed vellum (see Project Notes)
- Sheet of white paper
- 3 tall clear drinking glasses or clear candle holders
- 3 votive candles
- Clear tape or glue

*Stencil Magic stencils, stencil brushes, and adhesive; and Ceramcoat acrylic paints and Gleams paint from Delta.

Project Notes

Follow manufacturer's instructions for using stencils and other stenciling products. Refer to directions for stenciling under "Painting Techniques" in General Instructions, page 190.

Books of printed vellum pages are available in craft stores that carry scrapbooking supplies or "memory book" supplies.

Refer to photo throughout.

Wine Glass Rings

Keep wine glasses straight at your next holiday party with these wire-and-bead ID rings.
Your guests can take them home as a reminder of a wonderful night!

Designs by Samantha McNesby

Materials
Each Ring
- 5" 20-gauge gold or copper wire
- 6 (10/0) gold seed beads
- 2 (4mm) white pearl beads
- 1 large and 2 small beads of the same color
- Wire snips or craft scissors
- Needle-nose pliers

Project Note
Refer to photo throughout.

Instructions

1. Using needle-nose pliers, make a closed loop in one end of wire.

2. For each ring, string beads in this sequence: gold bead, small colored bead, gold bead, pearl, gold bead, large colored bead, gold bead,

pearl, gold bead, small colored bead, gold bead.

3. Wrap wire into circle about 1½" in diameter. **Note:** *Try wrapping the wire around a small bottle of acrylic*

craft paint; it is the perfect size for this project. Thread straight end of wire through loop and fold wire over to make a hook that will slide through loop. Trim off any excess wire. ✽

Frosty Votives

Instructions

1. Wrap plain paper around glass or candle holder to make a pattern for stenciled sleeve that will fit smoothly around glass. Using paper pattern, cut printed vellum to make a sleeve for each glass.

2. Hold stencil in place on vellum using only spray adhesive; do not use any type of tape. Do not remove backing from self-adhesive stencils; simply spray back with adhesive.

3. Stencil designs on papers:

Christmas stocking: Holly borders

are positioned around top and bottom, using green for leaves and red for berries and ribbon sections. Stocking is positioned in center of sleeve, using red for stocking, candy canes and holly berry; blue for heel and toe; white for cuff; green for leaves and old parchment for teddy bear.

Wreath: "Peace, Love, Joy" border is positioned around top, using gold; wreath is stenciled in center, using red for bow and berries, and green for remainder of wreath.

Santa's Sleigh: "Merry Christmas!" is stenciled at top using red. Santa's sleigh is stenciled in center, using red for hat and sleeves; white for pompom, hatband, beard and

cuffs; flesh for face; green for mittens; old parchment for sleigh runners and top trim; and blue for sleigh. Trees are stenciled on both sides of sleigh using green.

4. Carefully remove stencils from paper. Paper may appear to be a bit buckled, but it will be fine when placed around the glass.

5. When designs are dry, fasten stenciled paper sleeves around outside of glasses using clear tape or glue to secure edges of vellum together. Do not fasten vellum to glass, so stenciled sleeves can be changed as desired.

6. Insert a votive candle in each glass or candle holder. ✽

Flying Santa

Use this elegant painted box as a wintry decoration or to hold your most cherished Christmas ornaments.

Design by Joyce Atwood

Materials

- Wooden oval box*
- Heavy brown paper cut from paper bag
- Tack cloth
- Graphite paper
- 1¾" wooden snowflake cutout*
- Acrylic paints*: sand, Williamsburg blue, sable brown, burnt umber, lamp black, Black Forest green, mink tan, rookwood red, medium flesh, light cinnamon, deep midnight blue, Payne's gray, black plum, DeLane's cheek color, arbor green
- Multipurpose sealer*
- Foam brush
- Paintbrushes: ¼" angular; ⅜"; 2, 4 and 10 shaders; ¾" glaze/wash; size 0 liner; #4 and #6 rounds; ¼" comb; ½" filbert comb; 4, 6, 8 and 10 rounds
- Stencils*: snowflake and checkerboard
- Ultra-fine iridescent glitter*
- Matte spray*

Wooden box from Artist Club; snowflake cutout from Bear With Us; acrylic paints, multipurpose sealer and iridescent glitter and matte spray from DecoArt; snowflake stencil #BL-130 from American Traditional Stencils; and Simply Stencils checkerboard #28444 from Plaid.

Project Notes

Refer to photo and pattern throughout.

To transfer pattern, refer to instructions for "Using Transfer & Graphite Paper" in the General Instructions, page 190.

Refer to directions for base-coating, highlighting, dry-brushing and shading under "Painting Techniques" in the General Instructions, page 190.

Let all coats of paint, sealer and matte spray dry between applications unless otherwise instructed.

Instructions

1. Base-coat top of lid and sides and bottom of box with dark forest green mixed with an equal amount of multipurpose sealer. Base-coat edge of lid and interior of box with arbor green mixed with an equal amount of multipurpose sealer.

2. Sand inside and out with heavy brown paper; wipe off dust with tack cloth.

3. Transfer pattern for Santa and reindeer to center of box lid. Base-coat hat and coat with rookwood red; paint trim on hat and cuff arbor green.

4. Stencil partial snowflakes on hat and coat using sand paint; while paint is still wet, sprinkle with glitter.

5. *Shading:* With black plum, float around hat and all parts of coat except left side of coat closest to deer's leg and right sleeve on right side; highlight these areas with DeLane's cheek color. Shade cuff and hat trim with floats of dark forest green; add deep midnight blue stripes to trim.

6. *Pompom:* Base-coat with gray; using liner, pull out hairs with sand.

7. *Santa's gown:* Base-coat with tan; shade with burnt umber.

8. *Santa's face:* Base-coat with medium flesh; shade with cinnamon. Stipple cheeks with rookwood red. Float nose with cinnamon. Add eyes and eyelashes with black; highlight eyes with dots of sand. Add rookwood red mouth; highlight center of lip with DeLane's cheek color.

9. *Hair, mustache, eyebrows and beard:* Base-coat with gray; using comb brush and sand, form strands of hair. Add more hairs with sand and liner. Shade by floating under mustache with gray.

10. *Reindeer:* Base-coat body with burnt umber. Add nose with rookwood red and collar with deep midnight blue. Paint antlers sable brown and white of tail sand.

11. *Shading and highlighting:* Float around tail, legs, next to collar and on chin with black. Highlight top of head and ears with sable brown. Dry-brush sable brown on body, legs, head and tail. Highlight over ear tops with a float of tan; shade inside ears with black. Shade around antlers with burnt umber. Dry-brush highlight of tan on antlers. Shade nose next to face with black plum. Highlight end with DeLane's cheek color. Line mouth with black. Shade inside hooves with black; highlight

around them with tan. Shade sand part of tail next to brown part with tan. Shade around collar with gray. Highlight center of collar with Williamsburg blue.

12. *Shoe and mitten:* Base-coat shoe with black; float highlight of Williamsburg blue around it. Base-coat mitten with sable brown; shade with burnt umber; dry-brush highlight with tan.

13. *Snowflakes:* Base-coat wooden snowflake with sand. Add a second coat and while paint is still wet, sprinkle with glitter. Using snowflake stencil and sand, stencil snowflakes on box lid and sides and sprinkle with glitter while still wet.

14. Stencil two rows of rookwood red squares in a checkerboard pattern around side of lid. Shade top and bottom edges of lid side with dark forest green.

15. Spray painted surfaces with several coats of matte spray. ❅

Flying Santa

Holiday Memories Photo Mats

*Make everyday picture frames ready for holiday memories
with these beautifully detailed holly berry photo mats.*

Designs by Vicki Schreiner

Materials

- 2 (8" x 10") off-white photo mats with oval opening for 5" x 7" photos
- Woodburner with mini flow point*
- Pigment ink small stamp pads*: burgundy, green tea, bisque, misty mauve, sage
- Brush-tip applicators*
- Graphite paper
- Fine-grit sandpaper
- Needle-nose pliers
- Heat-resistant surface
- Removable tape
- Masking tape
- Ballpoint pen
- Cotton-tip swabs

Creative Woodburner #5567 with Mini Flow Point #5593 from Walnut Hollow; Versa Color Acid Free Pigment Ink stamp pads and Fantastix applicators from Tsukineko.

Project Notes

Refer to photo and patterns throughout.

See directions for transferring pattern under "Using Transfer & Graphite Paper" in the General Instructions, page 190. Do not transfer stippling dots; these are for your reference when shading.

Follow manufacturer's instructions for using woodburning tool, heeding safety precautions. Change

Holiday Memories Holly

tip to mini flow point and tighten with needle-nose pliers.

Before woodburning project, practice on a piece of scrap mat board. Hold tool like a pen and use slow, short, sketching strokes to try straight and curved lines. Using a tapping motion, try making clusters of stippled dots.

To maintain even heat flow, occasionally clean tool by dragging the tip across sandpaper.

Use a separate brush-tip applicator to apply each color of ink. Dab tip onto ink pad, then dab onto paper towel before touching tip to mat. Apply color using small, circular motion.

Woodburning

1. Transfer desired design to corner of mat board.

2. Using mini flow point, woodburn all outlines. For shading, burn clusters of stippled dots, making dots darker and denser in areas to be shaded more heavily.

Painting & Detailing

1. Lightly color in each area of design, using misty mauve for ribbons and bows and sage for leaves. For berries, apply burgundy around outside and blend toward center with cotton-tipped swab.

2. Shade ribbons and bows with burgundy and leaves with tea green using the same technique and softly blending shading color into original color. Using bisque and cotton-tipped swab, apply shading around outer edges of designs and oval opening.

3. Apply sage to beveled edge of oval opening. ❋

Holiday Memories Mistletoe

Christmas Paper Scrapbook

Give the gift of warm Christmas memories for years to come! This scrapbook can be personalized for everyone on your list by simply choosing a different wrapping paper.

Design by Nancy Marshall

Materials

- Illustration board
- Christmas wrapping paper (see Project Notes)
- Self-adhesive paper: 2 (8½" x 11") sheets to match or coordinate with wrapping paper (for inner covers), and a 4" square in a different coordinating color (for central motif on front cover)
- 8" x 10" paper for scrapbook pages
- 1 yard or more craft cord* to coordinate with wrapping paper (see Project Notes)
- Spray adhesive
- Thin tacky craft glue with brush
- ½" heart-shaped hole punch (or other shape as desired)
- ¼" round paper punch
- Craft drill with ¼" bit
- Mat knife
- Paper cutter (optional)

Needloft Craft Cord from Uniek.

Project Notes

Refer to photo and Figs. 1 and 2 throughout.

Use a heavy, high-quality wrapping paper for this project.

White/gold #55007 Needloft Craft Cord was used on sample project.

Instructions

1. From illustration board, cut two pieces 8" x 8¾" and two strips 1" x 8". From wrapping paper, cut two pieces 10" x 12". From each full sheet of self-adhesive paper, cut a piece 7½" x 9½".

2. *Covers:* Referring to Fig. 1, mark corner placements of illustration board pieces on wrong side of wrapping paper pieces. ***Note:*** *If paper design has a direction as on the sample project, make sure front and back covers will align.* Apply spray adhesive to each piece of illustration board and press it in place.

3. Referring to Fig. 2, brush glue at each corner and fold paper back. Working along short sides and then long ones, brush a ½" strip of glue at board edge and fold paper back onto it.

4. Center and adhere a 7½" x 9½" piece of self-adhesive paper inside each cover.

5. *Cover decoration:* Cut a single motif from a scrap of wrapping paper; glue it in center of a 4" square of self-adhesive paper. Punch four shapes (hearts on sample project) from same self-adhesive paper used for inside covers. Place one in each corner of 4" square. Affix square to center of front cover.

6. Drill two holes 5" apart and centered on small board section of each cover. Center a piece of filler paper on cover and mark positions of holes on it; use this as a guide to punch holes in pages.

7. Sandwich pages between covers, aligning holes. Wrap ends of plastic canvas cord with tape, then thread cord ends into holes from front cover though pages and through back cover. Cross ends of cord in back and thread ends back through opposite holes to front of scrapbook; tie cord in a bow. Trim off taped ends and tie each end in an overhand knot to prevent fraying. ❈

Christmas Gift Tags

Turn leftover scraps of paper and fabric into colorful tags for all the gifts under your tree!

Designs by Samantha McNesby

Materials

- Scraps of holiday fabrics
- Scraps of fusible webbing
- Card stock: white, ivory or parchment
- Decorative paper edgers
- Fine-point black marking pen
- Hole punch
- Embroidery floss to coordinate with fabric(s)
- Iron

Project Notes

Refer to photo throughout.

Refer to manufacturer's instructions for using fusible webbing.

Instructions

1. Fuse webbing to wrong side of fabric. Cut desired motifs from fused fabric.

2. Remove backing from fabric motif(s) and fuse to card stock.

Using marker, outline fabric with a dot-dash border.

3. Using decorative edgers, cut around fabric motif leaving a ¼" border of plain card stock.

4. Write to/from information on plain side of card. Punch hole at center top; thread through a loop made from an 8" length of embroidery floss. ❋

Christmas Paper Scrapbook

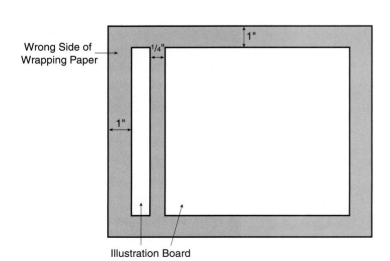

Wrong Side of Wrapping Paper

1"

¼"

1"

Illustration Board

Fig. 1

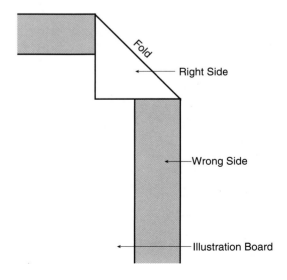

Fold

Right Side

Wrong Side

Illustration Board

Fig. 2

Mosaic Tile Gingerbread Frame

This gingerbread frame has the look of mosaic tile, but is created with the ease of painting!

Design by June Fiechter

Materials
- Black oval craft frame*
- Acrylic paints*: white wash, spice pink, olive green, lamp black, cherry red, winter blue, camel
- 3-dimensional lacquer*
- White transfer paper
- 10" piece ⅜"-wide red satin ribbon
- #4 paintbrush

Frame #PCF03 from Stampendous; Americana acrylic paints from DecoArt; and 3-D Crystal Lacquer from Sakura Hobby Craft.

Project Notes
To transfer pattern, refer to instructions for "Using Transfer & Graphite Paper" in the General Instructions, page 190.

When painting, take care to keep colors inside lines; the unpainted black areas of frame should look like black grout around the painted "tiles."

Refer to photo throughout.

Refer to manufacturer's instructions for assembling painted frame.

Instructions
1. Transfer pattern onto front of frame.

Mosaic Tile Gingerbread Frame

2. Paint every other tile in outermost row red; paint remaining tiles in that row olive green.

3. Paint gingerbread man's cheeks pink; paint buttons red; paint eyes and white trim on arms and legs white. Paint candy cane in alternating stripes of white and red. Paint remaining tiles of gingerbread man camel. Paint round candy in lower right corner in alternating stripes of red and white; paint wrapper ends white. Paint remaining tiles in middle of frame blue. Let dry.

4. Add black pupils over gingerbread man's white eyes; when dry, add tiny white highlight specks to pupils using the tip of toothpick or paintbrush handle. Let dry.

5. Squeeze a small amount of crystal lacquer onto center of each painted tile; spread lacquer to edges of tile without covering black "grout." Repeat with a second coat if desired.

6. Paint two dowels (from frame package) black. When dry, assemble frame as directed.

7. Thread ribbon through holes in top of frame and tie in bow; trim ribbon ends as desired. ❊

Cowboy Santa

Stitch fabric scraps to old denim to create this Western design to hold a loved one's goodies this Christmas!

Design by Chris Malone

Materials

- Recycled adult-size blue jeans
- Fabrics: ½ yard red bandanna print, 15" x 7" white-on-white print, 4" square mottled brown, scraps of tan, green, red-and-black check
- 1⅓ yards ¾"-wide braided jute trim
- ⅓ yard 2"-wide suede fringe trim*
- 4" x 6" fleece
- ¼ yard iron-on adhesive*
- Iron
- Size 5 black pearl cotton
- Buttons: red ½" shank button with shank removed, 1"–1¼" round tan button
- 2 (6mm) black cabochons
- ½" wooden furniture plug
- Dark rosy flesh acrylic paint
- Small paintbrush
- Pink powdered cosmetic blusher
- Cotton-tip swab
- 1" ⅜"-wide red grosgrain ribbon
- Fabric adhesive*
- Matching sewing threads
- Sewing machine (optional)
- Embroidery needle
- Seam sealant

Suede fringe trim from St. Louis Trimmings; HeatnBond Ultra Hold Iron-on Adhesive from Therm O Web; and Fabri-Tac Adhesive from Beacon.

Project Notes

Refer to photo and patterns throughout.

Follow manufacturer's instructions for using iron-on adhesive.

Before cutting fabric for stocking and lining, use a photocopier with enlarging capabilities to enlarge stocking pattern 200 percent.

Use ¼" seam allowance throughout.

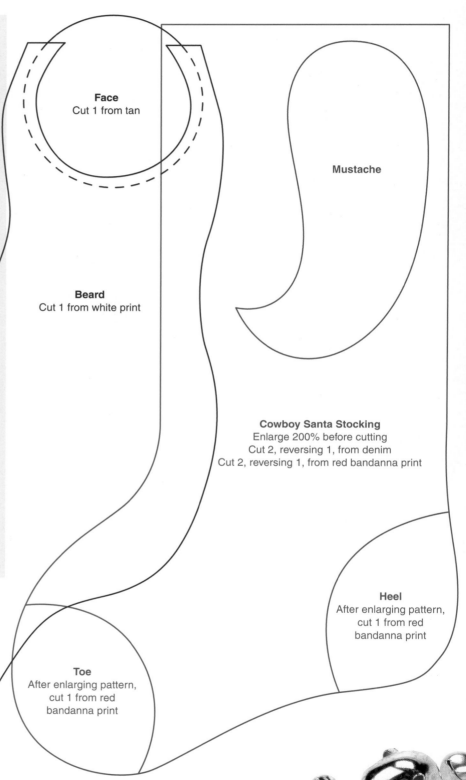

Face
Cut 1 from tan

Mustache

Beard
Cut 1 from white print

Cowboy Santa Stocking
Enlarge 200% before cutting
Cut 2, reversing 1, from denim
Cut 2, reversing 1, from red bandanna print

Heel
After enlarging pattern,
cut 1 from red
bandanna print

Toe
After enlarging pattern,
cut 1 from red
bandanna print

Instructions

1. Cut two stockings, reversing one, from blue jeans fabric and two, reversing one, from red bandanna print for lining.

2. Fuse iron-on adhesive to wrong side of brown, green, tan and red-and-black check fabrics; fuse additional adhesive to back of 6" x 4" piece of red bandanna print and 4½" x 7" piece of white-on-white print. Cut hat and brim from adhesive-backed brown fabric, two holly leaves from green, face from tan, hatband from red-and-black check, beard from white print, and stocking heel and toe from bandanna print. Arrange fabric pieces on front of stocking and fuse in place.

3. Using black pearl cotton, "sew" heel and toe to denim stocking along inner curved edges with large, primitive-style stitches.

4. Pin denim stocking front and back together, right sides facing. Sew around stocking, leaving it open at top. Clip curves; turn right side out.

5. *Lining:* Pin bandanna-print lining front and back together right sides facing and sew together, leaving top open. Clip curves but do not turn right side out. Turn and press ¼" hem at top. Slip lining inside stocking; match side seams. Slipstitch top of lining to top of stocking and cuff seams.

6. *Mustache:* Cut remaining unfused white print fabric in half. On wrong side of one piece, trace two mustaches, reversing one. Lay two pieces of white print fabric together, right sides facing and pattern on top; pin to fleece. Sew on traced lines through all layers. Cut out ⅛" from seam; clip curves. Cut slash through one layer of fabric only; turn mustaches right side out through slashes and press. Whipstitch slashes closed. Using pearl cotton, sew running stitch around mustaches ⅛" from edge.

Continued on page 37

Scottie Dog Throw

Warm up a loved one with this darling Scottie dog plush blanket.
Drape the throw over a chair for a holiday decoration that is both pretty and practical!

Design by Angie Wilhite

Materials

- 48" x 60" burgundy fleece blanket
- 6" x 12" white felt*
- 5" x 7" blue-and-gold plaid fabric
- Embroidery floss: gold, black
- Embroidery needle
- ¼ yard iron-on adhesive*
- ¼ yard pressing paper
- Iron

*Felt from Kunin; and HeatnBond
iron-on adhesive from Therm O Web.*

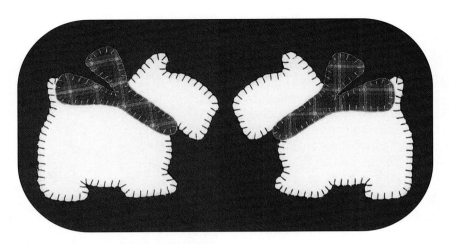

Project Notes

Refer to photo and patterns throughout.

Refer to manufacturer's instructions for using iron-on adhesive.

Instructions

1. Prewash blanket and plaid fabric without using fabric softener. Press to remove wrinkles.

2. Apply iron-on adhesive to wrong side of felt and plaid fabric. Trace two Scotties, reversing one, on paper side of white felt. Trace two scarves, reversing one, on paper side of plaid fabric.

3. Cut out shapes; remove paper backing and position Scottie dogs, then scarves, in one corner of blanket so dogs face each other. Cover design area with pressing paper and fuse with iron.

4. Using 2 strands black embroidery floss, blanket-stitch around white felt Scottie dogs. Using 2 strands gold floss, blanket-stitch around plaid scarves. ❊

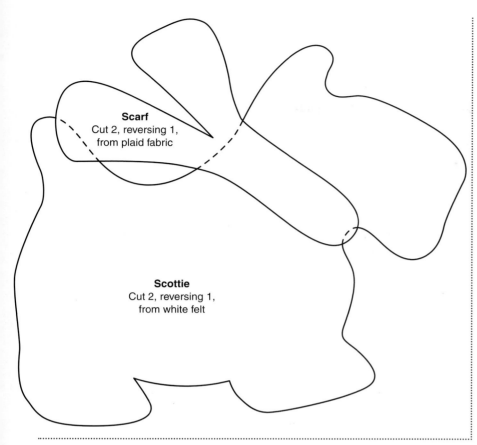

Scarf
Cut 2, reversing 1,
from plaid fabric

Scottie
Cut 2, reversing 1,
from white felt

8. *Back pocket:* Carefully cut pocket from jeans; cut fabric from back of pocket. Apply seam sealant to cut edges of ribbon; glue ribbon lengthwise along back edge of pocket on one side to resemble label. Apply glue to side and bottom edges of pocket; press onto back of stocking.

9. *Hanky:* Cut 5" square from bandanna print; fringe edges ⅜". Fold pleat diagonally down hanky and tuck into pocket, securing with glue if desired.

10. Working with about 4" at a time, apply glue to side seam of stocking, beginning 1" below top edge. Press jute trim into glue. Continue all around, ending 1" from top; cut off excess. Fold top of stocking down ¾" to expose red bandanna-print lining; glue in place. Starting at back where hanging loop will be attached, glue suede fringe to bottom of fold.

11. *Hanger:* Cut 6" piece of jute trim; apply seam sealant to ends and let dry. Fold trim into a loop and tack or glue ends to stocking back leaving 2" loop extending above stocking. Glue tan button over hanger to conceal ends of jute trim. ❁

Cowboy Santa

Continued from page 35

7. Using cotton swab, apply blusher to face for cheeks. Paint wooden plug rosy flesh for nose; let dry.

Glue cabochons in place for eyes. Glue mustache halves in place, slashed sides down; glue nose above and between mustache halves. Glue red button at base of holly leaves.

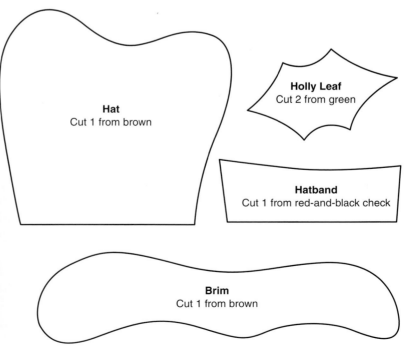

Hat
Cut 1 from brown

Holly Leaf
Cut 2 from green

Hatband
Cut 1 from red-and-black check

Brim
Cut 1 from brown

Holiday Puppets

Set the stage for an evening of fun with these easy-to-stitch felt characters! After the puppet show, you can hang them from a wall, or stuff them to sit on the edge of the mantel or a table.

Designs by Chris Malone

Materials

Santa

- Felt*: 2 (9" x 12") sheets red, black, white, small piece apricot, white plush
- Buttons: 2 (⅜") flat black, 1¼" flat back, ⅜" shank of any color
- 1" white pompom
- Sewing thread to match apricot felt

Reindeer

- Felt*: 2 (9" x 12") sheets cashmere tan, 2 (3") squares antique white, black and lime
- 3" square iron-on adhesive
- Buttons: ½" red shank, 2 (⅜") flat black
- ¾" red jingle bell
- Green sewing thread

Snowman

- Felt*: 2 (9" x 12") sheets white, ½ sheet black, 1" x 12" strip lime, small pieces red and orange
- Buttons: 2 (⅜") flat black, 3 (⅞") flat black
- 2 (1") bright blue pompoms
- 6" 18-gauge black plastic-coated wire

Each Puppet

- Black embroidery floss
- Embroidery and hand-sewing needles
- Craft glue
- Sewing machine (optional)
- Freezer paper (optional)
- Iron

Felt from Kunin.

Project Notes

Refer to photo and patterns throughout.

Use 2 strands black floss for all stitching unless instructed otherwise.

If desired, instead of hand-stitching puppets together, machine-stitch ⅛"–¼" from edge on right side of felt.

Patterns are sized to fit smaller hands. Use photocopier to enlarge patterns 110–120 percent for adult hands.

To cut small pieces of felt easily and accurately, trace patterns onto dull side of freezer paper; cut apart leaving small margin around lines. Place paper shiny side down on felt and press with iron for about 3 seconds. Paper will stay in place. Cut out on traced lines, cutting through paper and felt. Remove paper and reuse once more, if desired.

Santa

1. Cut pieces from felt: *red*—two Santa hats and two bodies, cutting on solid lines; *regular white*—four Santa mustaches and two beards; *apricot*—one Santa face and one Santa nose; *black*—four mittens and four legs.

2. Pin legs together in pairs and blanket-stitch around edges. Pin or lightly glue tops of legs ⅜" inside bottom edge of front of Santa's body.

3. Lightly apply glue to ¼" at ends of arms on Santa front; press flat ends of mittens into glue so mittens overlap ends of arms. Repeat on back of Santa.

4. Sew ⅜" black buttons to Santa face for eyes; pin or lightly glue face to front of head.

5. Blanket-stitch along bottom of front, catching tops of legs in stitches. Without clipping floss, pin front and back together, wrong sides facing, and blanket-stitch all around puppet. Blanket-stitch bottom edge of back only to finish.

6. Hold beards together and blanket-stitch around edges; repeat with mustaches, sewing them together in pairs. Glue beard to bottom of face.

7. Using matching thread, sew gathering stitches around edge of apricot circle for nose; place shank button on center of felt circle and pull gathering stitches to gather felt around shank; knot thread ends. Sew felt-covered button to face for nose; glue mustaches under nose.

8. Blanket-stitch hats together, leaving bottom open. Slip hat onto head and glue lightly. Glue pompom to tip of hat.

9. From white plush felt cut 7" x ½" piece for hat trim and two 3½" x ½" pieces for trim around wrists. Starting in center back, apply glue to felt strip and press to cover edges of hat or mittens. Trim as necessary, butting ends together neatly to finish.

10. Sew large black button to front of Santa's suit.

Reindeer

1. Sandwich iron-on adhesive between antique white felt squares and iron to fuse layers together.

2. Cut pieces from felt: *tan*—two reindeer bodies, cutting on dashed lines; four reindeer legs, four ears and two heads; *fused antique white*—two antlers; *black*—six hooves; *lime*—one reindeer bow.

3. Lightly glue two hooves to bottoms of two legs for leg fronts. Pin front and back legs together in pairs; blanket-stitch around edges. Pin or lightly glue tops of legs ⅜" inside bottom edge of front of reindeer's body.

4. Lightly apply glue to ¼" at ends of arms on reindeer front; press flat ends of hooves into glue so hooves overlap ends of arms. Repeat on back of reindeer.

5. Blanket-stitch along bottom of front, catching tops of legs in stitches. Without clipping floss, pin front and back together, wrong sides facing, and blanket-stitch all around puppet. Blanket-stitch bottom edge of back only to finish.

6. Sew ⅜" black buttons to one reindeer face for eyes; embroider two straight stitches over buttons for eyebrows and backstitch down center of face. Sew red shank button in place for nose.

7. Pin ears together in pairs; blanket-stitch around edges. Pin face front and back together, wrong sides facing. Insert edges of ears and ends of antlers between edges of face. Blanket-stitch around face, catching ears and antlers as you stitch.

8. Fold back ends of bow, matching narrow areas to center of strip. Using matching thread, gather center of bow; knot thread and sew jingle bell to center bottom of bow.

9. Glue head to front of puppet, matching top edges. Glue bow and bell under head at an angle.

Snowman

1. Cut pieces from felt: *white*—two bodies, cutting on solid lines; *red*—four mittens; *orange*—two snowman noses; *black*—four legs and 7" x ½" strip.

2. Pin legs together in pairs and blanket-stitch around edges. Pin or lightly glue tops of legs ⅜" inside bottom edge of front of snowman's body.

3. Lightly apply glue to ¼" at ends of arms on snowman front; press flat ends of mittens into glue so mittens overlap ends of arms. Repeat on back of snowman.

4. Sew ⅜" black buttons to snowman face for eyes; straight-stitch two eyebrows and backstitch smile.

5. Blanket-stitch along bottom of front, catching tops of legs in stitches. Without clipping floss, pin front and back together, wrong sides facing, and blanket-stitch all around puppet. Blanket-stitch bottom edge of back only to finish.

6. Cut 7" strip of black felt in half to make two 3½" strips for wrist trim. Starting in center back, apply glue to felt strip and press to cover edges of mittens. Trim as necessary, butting ends together neatly to finish.

7. Sew large black buttons down center front of snowman. Wrap lime strip around neck for scarf; tie at side and lightly glue overlapped ends in place. Clip ends in ½" fringe.

8. Hold noses together and blanket-stitch around edges; glue nose to face with tip of nose overlapping scarf.

9. *Earmuffs:* Shape wire into a curve to fit over top of head; tack and/or glue ends to side of face. Glue pom-poms over ends of wire. ❋

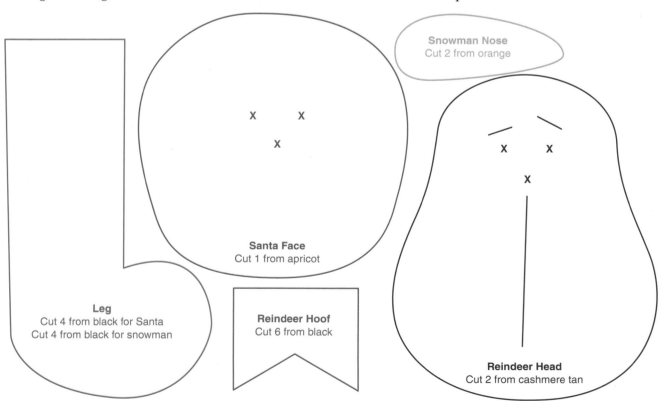

Snowman Nose
Cut 2 from orange

Santa Face
Cut 1 from apricot

Leg
Cut 4 from black for Santa
Cut 4 from black for snowman

Reindeer Hoof
Cut 6 from black

Reindeer Head
Cut 2 from cashmere tan

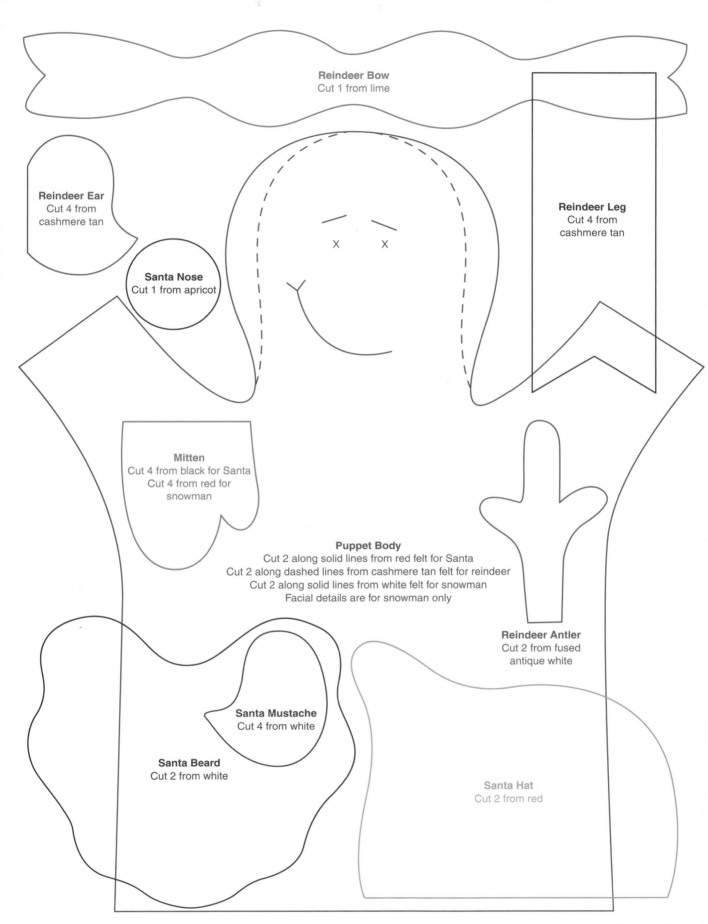

Reindeer Bow
Cut 1 from lime

Reindeer Ear
Cut 4 from
cashmere tan

Reindeer Leg
Cut 4 from
cashmere tan

Santa Nose
Cut 1 from apricot

Mitten
Cut 4 from black for Santa
Cut 4 from red for
snowman

Puppet Body
Cut 2 along solid lines from red felt for Santa
Cut 2 along dashed lines from cashmere tan felt for reindeer
Cut 2 along solid lines from white felt for snowman
Facial details are for snowman only

Reindeer Antler
Cut 2 from fused
antique white

Santa Mustache
Cut 4 from white

Santa Beard
Cut 2 from white

Santa Hat
Cut 2 from red

Holly Berry Frame

This large glass frame will elegantly hold your most precious Christmas memory.
The delightful holly and berries will attractively decorate your home for the season.

Design by Carol van Tol for Delta Technical Coatings

Materials

- 8" x 10" glass picture frame*
- Craft knife
- "Frosted" paints*: really red, kiwi
- Leading paint*
- Surface conditioner*

Frame from Provo Craft; and PermEnamel Frosted Looks paints, Liquid Lead Glass Paint and surface conditioner from Delta.

Project Notes

Refer to photo and pattern throughout. Before reproducing pattern, use a photocopier with enlarging capabilities to enlarge it 125 percent.

Refer to manufacturer's instructions for using PermEnamel products.

Instructions

1. Clean front of frame with surface conditioner.

2. Tape pattern to back of frame.

3. Paint scrolls with liquid leading: Apply leading directly from tip of bottle; start by painting long scroll along each edge first, squeezing slowly and evenly to get a consistent line of leading. **Note:** *Mistakes can be wiped off quickly with surface conditioner; or, wait until it dries and scrape it off with a craft knife.* Then add leaves, berries and smaller scrolls. Finally, paint small scallops

around edge. Let dry completely.

4. Fill scallops and holly leaves with two coats kiwi paint. Fill berries with two coats really red.

5. Let frame dry completely. Scratch off any mistakes with craft knife. Remove pattern and clean frame with glass cleaner. ❊

Holly Berry Frame
Enlarge 125%

Christmas Home Decor

Deck the halls and walls with festive Christmas crafts! This cheerful chapter brings you dozens and dozens of merry decorating ideas for every room in your home—perfect for bringing on that Christmas spirit of joy!

Plush Snowman

With his plump body and rosy cheeks, this huggable snowman is ready to steal your heart!

Design by Sandy Dye

Materials

- Felt*: 1 yard white plush; ⅓ yard each cranberry, hunter green and cardinal
- 6 whole cloves
- Red ½" bead
- 2 (3mm) black beads
- 2" x 36" torn strip of fabric
- Polyester fiberfill
- ½ yard jute twine
- Dried botanicals and moss
- 6" bird
- 4 assorted buttons
- White 6-strand embroidery floss and embroidery needle
- Pink powdered cosmetic blusher
- Cotton-tip swab (optional)
- Hot-glue gun

Felt from CPE.

Instructions

1. *Head:* Cut 7" x 16" piece white plush felt. Right sides facing, stitch together along 7" edges. Turn right side out. Thread needle with all 6 strands of floss; sew gathering stitch ¼" from one edge; pull tightly to gather and close end; knot floss ends and trim. Repeat along other edge, stuffing head with fiberfill before gathering thread and tying off.

2. *Body:* Cut 14" x 38" piece white plush felt. Right sides facing, stitch together along 14" edges. Turn right side out. Gather edges and stuff as described in step 1.

3. Cut six 1½-yard lengths of floss. Beginning at top of larger ball (one gathered end), vertically wrap floss around ball and repeat twice to make a total of six equal sections, pumpkin-style. Tie off. Repeat with

smaller ball, wrapping twice to create four sections. Glue smaller ball atop larger one.

4. *Arms:* Cut 6" x 9" piece of white plush felt. Right sides facing, fold in half lengthwise; using scissors, round off one end to create hand. Stitch from hand up to shoulder; turn right side out and stuff. Glue arm in place. Cut an 8" piece of jute twine; tie around wrist in a bow. Repeat to make a second arm.

5. *Jacket:* Cut 12" x 34" piece cranberry red felt; fold in half lengthwise. Round off bottom corners of jacket. Measure down 3" from top and 8" in from front opening on each side (short edges of jacket) and mark for armhole placement. Cut an X at each point just large enough to squeeze arm through. Fold back "collar" on each side and tack down with glue.

6. *Bow:* Fray torn edges of fabric

strip with pin; place fabric around neck, adjusting excess felt in back and gathering to accommodate neck. Tie in a pretty bow. (Have patience at this point until you achieve a nice fit.)

7. *Hat:* Cut 10" circle from hunter green felt. Sew gathering stitch 3" from edge. Place hat on head and pull gathering thread to size, then tie off. Stuff crown of hat lightly with fiberfill; glue hat to head. Glue moss around crown; add dried botanicals and bird.

8. *Face:* Mark position of eyes; stitch black beads in place, stitching from back of head to front to indent eyes. Glue on red bead for nose; glue on cloves to form snowman's smile. Add a bit of blusher to snowman's cheeks with swab or fingertip.

9. Glue arms down to jacket, adding a few dried flowers under arms. Glue buttons down center front. ✳

Baby Blitzen

Displaying this delightful reindeer on a tabletop for decoration will evoke oohs and ahhs from your holiday visitors.

Design by Debra Arch

Materials

- Felt: ⅓ yard taupe "shaggy," dark brown, black
- 2 (8mm) black pearls or beads
- 18mm silver jingle bell
- Polyester fiberfill
- 18" 18-gauge wire
- 15" green Christmas garland
- Dried Spanish moss
- 12" heavy tapestry cord or string
- 24" 4mm red metallic pearls on a string
- 1 yard ½"-wide silver wired ribbon
- Powdered cosmetic blusher or pink chalk
- Pinking shears
- Hand-sewing needle and taupe, brown and black sewing threads
- Sewing machine (optional)
- Wire cutters
- Fabric glue
- Dried German statice (optional)

Project Notes

Refer to photo and patterns throughout.

Use ¼" seam allowance throughout.

After sewing, use the tip of a straight pin to fluff up any nap from shaggy felt caught in seams.

Instructions

1. *Body:* From shaggy felt, cut two body pieces, one bottom and two 9" x 2½" rectangles for legs.

2. With right sides facing and using taupe thread, sew bodies together along sides and top only; sew bottom circle to bottom of body, leaving 4" opening. Turn body right side out and stuff the top 4" (head area) firmly; stuff remainder of body less firmly to give reindeer a huggable feel. Stitch opening closed.

3. *Head and neck:* Snugly tie heavy cord around body about 4" from top to define head and neck area. Sew jingle bell to nose tip. Using black thread, sew on black pearls for eyes.

4. *Antlers:* Cut two 1" x 14" strips dark brown felt. Align strips and, sewing by hand or machine, stitch ¼" from edge down length. Insert 18-gauge wire between strips, positioning it very close to stitching. *Note: About 2" of wire will extend beyond felt at each end.* Sew very close to wire along other side to encase wire in felt. *Tip: A zipper foot on the sewing machine works great to stitch very close to the wire.* Using pinking shears, cut seam allowances to ⅛" on each side of wire to form "jagged" antler effect.

5. *Attach antlers:* Insert 2" wire ends of antlers through head, placing them just above neck cord and poking them completely through head and out underside of head (chin area). Trim wire ends short with wire cutters.

6. Bend and twist antlers into desired position. Glue a small amount of Spanish moss at base of antlers for hair. Blush reindeer's cheeks with blusher or pink chalk applied with fingertip.

7. *Legs:* Right sides facing, fold 9" x 2½" felt rectangle in half to form 4½" x 2½" rectangle; sew along long sides. Turn right side out. Repeat with other rectangle to make second leg.

8. *Hooves:* Cut two 2½" x 3" pieces black felt. Fold one rectangle in half; sew up sides. Turn inside out. Insert leg and glue hoof to bottom of leg. Repeat for other hoof and leg.

9. Stuff only bottom 2½" of each leg. Fold ¼" seam allowance to inside at top of each leg and glue or sew top of each leg closed. Sew or glue legs to front of reindeer.

10. *Garland:* Wrap red pearls around garland. Wrap garland around reindeer's head and over neck cord; glue in place. Form ribbon into a bow; glue to garland off to one side. Securely glue underside of head down toward body to conceal wire ends of antlers. Insert small amounts of dried statice around garland as desired and glue in place. ❈

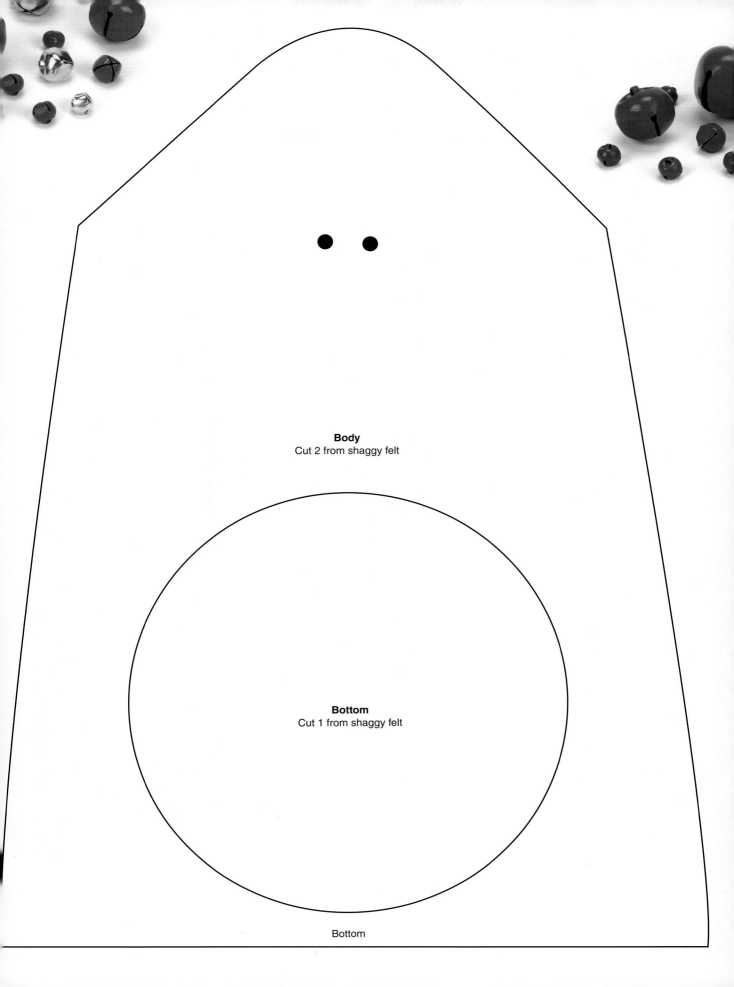

Body
Cut 2 from shaggy felt

Bottom
Cut 1 from shaggy felt

Bottom

Sleeping Angel

Rest easily with the gentle chiming of tin snowflakes dangling from this sleeping angel wind chime.

Design by Joyce Atwood

Materials

- "Rusted" wind chime*
- Acrylic paints*: snow white, tangerine, burnt orange, lamp black, Black Forest green, true ochre, Napa red, deep midnight blue, tomato red, DeLane's cheek color, arbor green
- Paintbrushes: ¼" and ⅜" angular; #2, #4 and #10 shaders; ¾" glaze/wash; size 0 and 1 liners; #4, #6, #8 and #10 rounds; ½" filbert comb
- Sea sponge
- ⅞"-wide and 1⅜"-wide snowflake stencils
- Matte spray*
- Coarse, lint-free cloth or towel
- White graphite paper

Wind chime by Kathy Steph's Folk Art; Americana acrylic paint and matte spray from DecoArt.

Project Notes

Refer to photo and pattern throughout.

To transfer pattern, refer to instructions for "Using Transfer & Graphite Paper" in the General Instructions, page 190.

Refer to directions for base-coating, highlighting, dry-brushing, shading and stenciling under "Painting Techniques" in General Instructions, page 190.

Let matte spray and paints dry between applications.

Preparation

1. Rub excess rust from wind chime using coarse cloth. Spray wind chime with two coats of matte spray.

2. Using sponge, apply midnight blue paint to cylinder of wind chime, leaving edges unpainted and allowing some rusty surface to show through paint. Repeat with snow white paint.

3. When dry, transfer pattern onto wind chime.

Painting

1. Stipple angel's hands, feet and face with snow white.

2. Base-coat robe with tomato red; float highlights of DeLane's cheek color on gown and float shading with Napa red. Add lines to gown with DeLane's cheek color.

3. Paint hat and cuffs on gown Black Forest green. Highlight top of hat and top of ribbed hat brim by floating with arbor green.

4. Paint nose burnt orange; float highlight of tangerine across top of nose. Add mouth and eyes with black. Shade around face, hands and feet with a float of deep midnight blue. Dry-brush cheeks with DeLane's cheek color.

Continued on page 52

Hugs for Mom Sled

Remember the love of your little ones with this painted snow baby and mom.
Hang the sled on a wall or display it on an end table in your living room.

Design by Joyce Atwood

Materials

- 16¼" L x 4⅞" W x 1¾" D wooden sled*
- Acrylic paints*: sand, burnt orange, lamp black, Black Forest green, rookwood red, black green, black plum, milk chocolate, DeLane's cheek color, French vanilla, camel, arbor green, admiral blue
- Paintbrushes: ¼" angular; ⅜"; #2, #4 and #10 shaders; ¾" glaze/wash; size 0 and 1 liners; #4, #6, #8 and #10 rounds; small stencil brush
- Stencil for ¾" checkerboard pattern
- Matte varnish*
- White graphite paper and pencil

Wooden sled from Artist Club; Americana acrylic spray and matte varnish from DecoArt.

Project Notes

Refer to photo and pattern throughout.

To transfer pattern, refer to instructions for "Using Transfer & Graphite Paper" in General Instructions, page 190.

Refer to directions for base-coating, highlighting, dry-brushing, shading and stenciling under "Painting Techniques" in General Instructions, page 190.

Let all coats of paint and varnish dry between applications.

Instructions

1. Base-coat sled runners and cross-pieces underneath with camel. Base-coat sled's center panel with admiral blue.

2. Transfer pattern to center panel using pencil and white graphite paper.

3. Using camel, base-coat snowlady's head, hat, mittens, snowbaby's head and boots, trim at bottom of snowlady's coat, her boots and star. Base-coat lady's coat with rookwood red and baby's coat with Black Forest green; base-coat baby's mittens and hat with arbor green.

4. Shade baby and lady's heads and boots with milk chocolate. Add burnt orange noses; shade noses with rookwood red and highlight along top edge with camel. Dot on

Hugs for Mom Sled

eyes and mouths using stylus dipped in black; highlight eyes with tiny specks of sand and paint eyebrows and eye-lashes with black.

5. Shade lady's hat with milk chocolate; dry-brush French vanilla highlights and add Black Forest green dots to crown and stripes to brim. Shade her coat with black plum; dry-brush highlights with DeLane's cheek color. Dot on camel buttons. Shade edges of coat trim at bottom with milk chocolate; add rookwood red checks to trim, and separate trim from coat with thin stripe of arbor green. Shade her mittens with milk chocolate and dry-brush highlights of French vanilla; add rookwood red stripes, highlighted with DeLane's cheek color. Add

stripe of arbor green at collar.

6. Shade baby's coat with black green and add dry-brushed high-lights of arbor green. Add a stripe of rookwood red at cuff; dry-brush highlight on stripe with DeLane's cheek color. Add wavy stripe at bot-tom of baby's coat with camel. Shade mittens and hat with Black Forest green; dry-brush highlights with sand. Stipple pompom at tip of hat with arbor green and Black Forest green. Add camel zigzag trim to baby's mitten and add specks of camel to hat brim.

7. Shade left edge of star with milk chocolate; highlight right side with sand. Stipple snow under lady's feet with sand.

8. Stencil rookwood red squares in a checkerboard pattern on outer surfaces of sled runners.

9. Spray sled with several coats of matte varnish. ❋

Sleeping Angel

Sleeping Angel

Continued from page 50

5. Paint moon with true ochre. Shade nose next to snow angel with burnt sienna. Highlight bot-tom of moon with a mixture of true ochre and snow white.

6. Using angle brush, float snow white along wing lines.

7. Using stencil brush and snow white, randomly stencil snowflakes of different sizes over surface of wind chime.

8. Stipple both sides of tin snowflake that dangles from wind chime with snow white, allowing some rust to show through paint.

Shade by floating the right edge on each side with deep midnight blue.

9. Spray painted wind chime with matte spray. ❋

52   *Big Book of Christmas Crafts*

Holly Switch Cover

Replace your ordinary light-switch cover with this colorful mosaic-look painted cover for the holidays!

Design by June Fiechter

Materials

- Porcelain single light-switch cover*
- Glossy acrylic paints*: gloss black, buttermilk, orange, Christmas red, hunter, sable brown, country blue, yellow green
- Paintbrushes: #3/0 spotter, ¾" wash
- White graphite paper

Switch cover from Design Works; Ultra Gloss Acrylic Enamel paints from DecoArt.

Project Notes

Refer to pattern, color key and photo throughout.

To transfer pattern, refer to instructions for "Using Transfer & Graphite Paper" in General Instructions, page 190.

When painting, take care to keep colors inside lines; the unpainted black areas of frame should look like black grout around the painted "tiles."

Let all applications of paints dry between coats. Follow manufacturer's instructions for using paints.

Instructions

1. Paint front and side edges of light-switch cover gloss black with ¾" brush.

2. Transfer pattern to front of light-switch cover with transfer paper.

3. Using spotter, paint "tiles" as directed by color key.

4. Using country blue, paint a wavy outline around switch plate on raised outer edge. ❖

COLOR KEY
B Gloss black
O Orange
R Christmas red
H Hunter
S Sable brown
C Country blue
Y Yellow green
　 Paint uncoded areas
　 with buttermilk

Candle Garden

With simple woodburning and painting, you can create this plate for a decorative place to burn your favorite holiday candles!

Designs by Deborah Brooks

Materials

- 12" wooden charger
- 7 (1½") wooden doll head beads
- Woodburner with multipurpose point
- Gold-leafing pen*
- Fine sandpaper
- Tack cloth
- Graphite paper
- Purple acrylic paint
- Glossy acrylic sealer
- ¾" flat paintbrush
- Assorted ecru pillar candles
- 2 cards Christmas Bell Design Stickers*
- Craft glue

Gold-leafing pen from Krylon; and Class A'Peels stickers from Mark Enterprises.

Project Notes

Refer to photo and pattern throughout.

Use photocopier to enlarge pattern 110 percent before transferring.

To transfer pattern, refer to instructions for "Using Transfer & Graphite Paper" in the General Instructions, page 190.

Follow manufacturer's instructions for using woodburning tool.

Candles are for decorative purposes only. Remove the stickers from candles as candles burn, and *never* leave burning candles unattended.

Let all coats of paint, gold leaf and acrylic sealant dry between applications.

Instructions

1. Sand wooden plate; wipe with tack cloth. Transfer design to center of plate.

2. Using point on woodburning tool, burn outline onto plate.

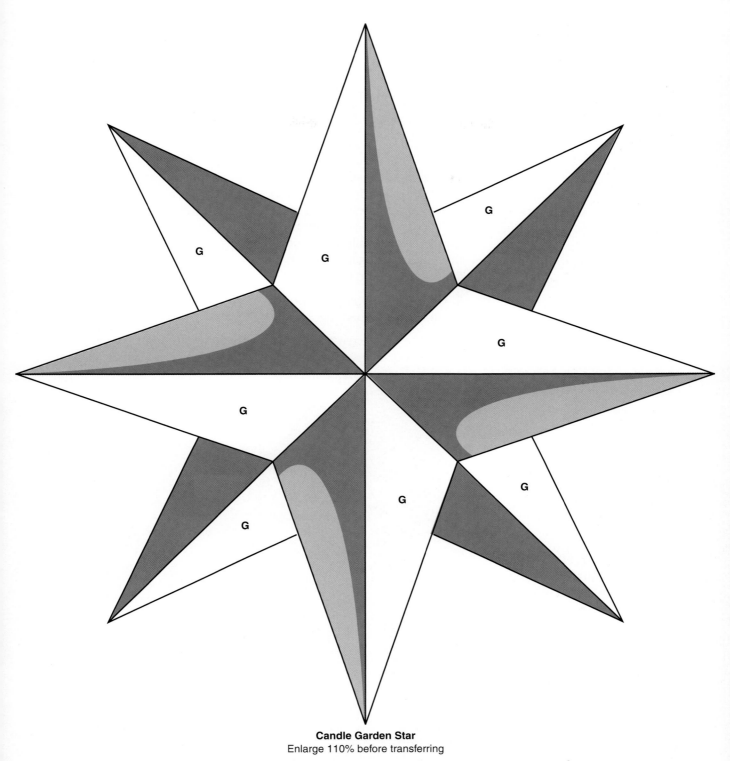

Candle Garden Star
Enlarge 110% before transferring

Shade alternating halves of star points with woodburning tool: On top layer, concentrate darkest color along center edges and in points at center of star. On bottom layer, fill in the shaded portions more completely.

3. Completely fill in other halves of star points, indicated by "G" on pattern, with gold-leafing pen.

4. Paint wooden balls and center portion of plate purple.

5. Dilute purple paint with an equal amount of water and paint outer rim and underside of plate with mixture.

6. Using gold-leafing pen, paint line around edge of plate and inner band between rim and plate center.

7. Spacing beads evenly, glue them around bottom of plate for ball feet.

8. Spray all surfaces of plate and feet with several coats of acrylic sealant.

9. Randomly apply stars from sheets of stickers to pillar candles. Arrange candles on plate. ❊

Santa & Snowman Picture

With a vibrant rub-on transfer, even the most inexperienced crafter can create this classic-looking picture to hang on a wall in your home.

Design by Shelia Sommers

Materials

- 8½" x 10½" wooden plaque*
- Acrylic paints*: periwinkle blue, Moroccan red
- #14 flat paintbrush
- Foil products*: foil adhesive, gold foil
- Spray gloss varnish*
- "Santa and Friends" rub-on transfer*
- Wooden craft stick (optional)
- 80- to 100-grit sandpaper
- Tack cloth
- Wood sealer

Walnut Hollow #1880 wooden plaque; Ceramcoat acrylic paints, Renaissance Foil products and varnish from Delta; and E-Z Rub-On Transfer from Royal.

Project Notes

Let all applications of wood sealer, paint and varnish dry between coats unless instructed otherwise.

Refer to manufacturers' instructions for applying transfer and foil products.

Instructions

1. Sand plaque; wipe off dust with tack cloth. Apply a coat of wood sealer; when dry, sand lightly.

2. Paint all surfaces of plaque Moroccan red, using sufficient coats to produce an opaque color.

3. On the right side of the plaque, lightly pencil a 5" x 6½" oval in the center. Paint oval blue.

4. Using scissors, separate sections of transfer, leaving ⅛" margin around each. Carefully remove protective sheeting from back of

Santa and snowman. Place design sticky side down on blue oval. Firmly rub surface of design with craft stick or the back of a paintbrush handle. Carefully lift the plastic sheeting, checking to be sure that design has adhered to plaque.

5. Using the same process, add greenery and berries around edge of oval.

6. Apply a heavy coat of foil adhesive to beveled edge of plaque; let dry completely. ***Note:*** *Adhesive will appear clear, not milky, when dry.*

7. Cut several wide strips of gold foil. Place one strip shiny side up onto dried adhesive. Use your finger or the end of a brush handle to firmly rub over the foil. Foil will adhere to dry adhesive as you lift the plastic sheeting. Repeat to foil entire edge of plaque to which adhesive was applied.

8. Spray all surfaces of plaque with several coats of varnish, allowing each coat to dry for 20–30 minutes before applying another. ❋

Wire Noel

Spell out your holiday greetings with bright red wire for display in your home!

Design by Joan Fee

Materials

- Red wire*: 14-gauge and 24-gauge
- Wire cutters
- Round-nose pliers
- Red metallic star garland
- 2 small nails

Wire from Artistic Wire.

Project Note

Refer to photo throughout.

Instructions

1. Cut four 12" pieces and one 28" piece of 14-gauge wire. Using your fingers and the round-nose pliers, free-form the letters N, O, E and L from 12" pieces.

2. *Hanger bar:* Fold 28" piece of wire in half and twist together, forming a small loop at fold. At opposite end, twist a matching loop using pliers. Wrap hanging bar with star garland.

3. *Letter hangers:* Cut four 8" pieces of 24-gauge wire. Wrap one end of an 8" piece of 24-gauge wire around the top of one letter; wrap other end around hanger bar. Repeat to hang letters so that they spell "NOEL."

4. Hang from nails through loops. ❄

Mitten Minder

Craft this handy snowman to hang your little ones' mittens to dry after playing in the snow.

Design by Barbara Matthiessen

Materials
- 12" x 6" x 1" pine stock
- 4 (1¼") wooden mittens, ¼" x 3" wooden rectangle*
- 11" x 10½" rustic fence*
- Wooden craft stick
- 4 wooden spring clothespins
- Acrylic paints*: white, black, real red, kelly green, pumpkin, valentine pink
- Paintbrushes
- Small stencil brush
- Fabric adhesive*
- Glossy acrylic coating*
- ½ sheet red felt
- 2 yards 3mm red satin ribbon
- 20 brass tacks
- 2 (⅝") 4-hole flat black buttons
- Craft wire: 10" 14-gauge silver, 3 yards 18-gauge black
- 3" x 14" torn strip plaid fabric
- Black embroidery floss
- Embroidery needle
- Black fine-tip permanent marker
- Craft saw
- Craft drill with 1⁄16" and ½" bits
- Sandpaper
- Graphite paper
- Sawtooth hanger or additional wire
- Hammer

Wooden mittens and rectangle from Lara's Crafts; fence from Walnut Hollow; Apple Barrel acrylic paints from Plaid; Fabri-Tac adhesive from Beacon; and glossy acrylic coating from Krylon.

Project Notes

Refer to patterns throughout.

To transfer patterns, refer to instructions for "Using Transfer & Graphite Paper" in the General Instructions, page 190.

Allow paints, ink and acrylic coating to dry between applications according to manufacturers' instructions.

Cutting & Painting

1. Cut snowman and two skate boots from pine stock. Using ½" bit, drill holes at shoulders and near bottom of snowman; drill a hole completely through top of each boot. Using 1⁄16" bit, drill two ¼"–½" holes up into bottom edge of each boot.

2. Paint all surfaces of snowman and wooden rectangle (sign) white; paint skate boots black; paint two wooden mittens red and two green.

3. Transfer lettering to sign and facial details to snowman.

4. Using a small amount of pink paint applied with stencil brush, blush cheeks. Paint nose pumpkin and eyes black.

5. Using black marker, add lettering and snowflakes to sign, mouth and outlines to snowman, and ribbing and details to mittens, reversing one or two mittens as desired.

Snowman & Sign Assembly

1. Sand edges of painted skate boots; glue craft stick to back of sign.

2. Attach buttons down center of snowman by nailing a brass tack through each of buttons' holes.

3. For lacing "hooks" on skate boots, hammer six brass tacks halfway into each boot where indicated, three on each side of boot.

4. Apply two coats of acrylic coating to all wooden pieces.

5. Cut four mittens from red felt. Using black floss, blanket-stitch mittens together in pairs.

6. Cut black 18-gauge wire into two 30" pieces and two 24" pieces. Curl one 30" piece around paintbrush handle or wooden spoon, leaving about 1½" straight at each end. Apply glue to one end and insert in hole in left shoulder; apply glue to other end and insert between felt layers into center of mitten. Repeat with remaining 30" wire to make snowman's right arm. Bend wire inside right mitten around craft stick so snowman holds sign; glue sign in place.

7. Curl 24" wires around paintbrush handle or wooden spoon for legs; glue one end in hole in bottom of snowman and thread other end through top of skate boot from front to back; twist wire end around itself to hold boot in place.

8. Cut silver 14-gauge wire in half. Bend each piece into a very shallow U-shape and glue ends in holes in bottoms of skate boots to make skate blades.

9. Cut ribbon in half. Use each piece to "lace up" one of the boots, crisscrossing it around tacks and tying ends in a bow.

10. Tie fabric strip around snowman's neck for scarf.

Finishing

1. Position snowman so that he "sits" on fence's bottom crosspiece; glue in place.

2. Glue clothespins to crosspieces about 1" from ends with clasps pointing down. Glue a wooden mitten to each clothespin.

3. Nail sawtooth hanger to back of fence or attach hanging loop of wire through holes in top crosspiece. ❅

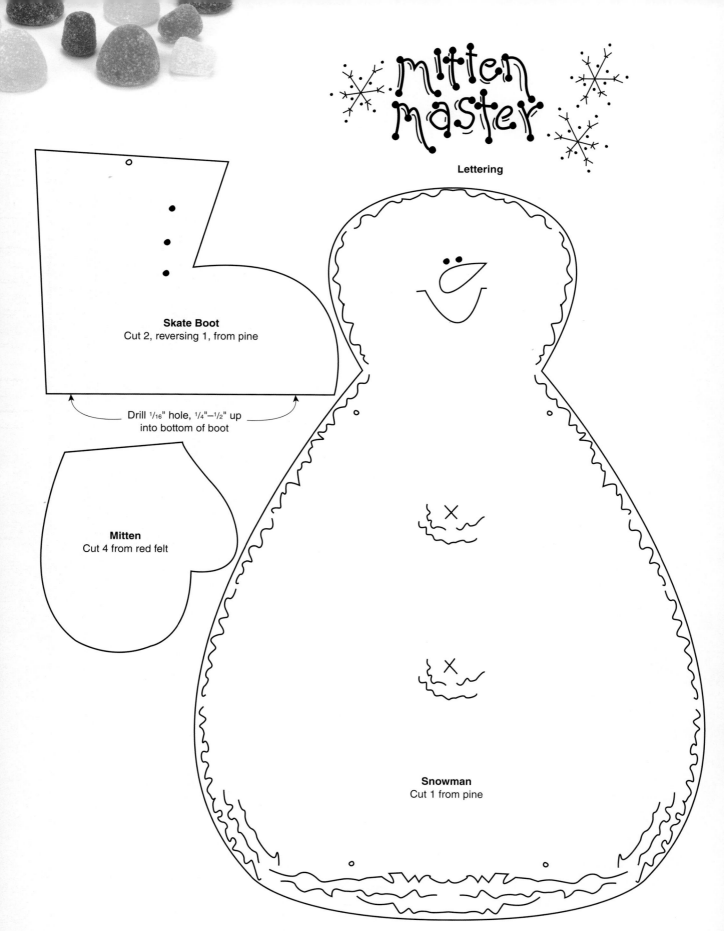

mitten master

Lettering

Skate Boot
Cut 2, reversing 1, from pine

Drill ¹/₁₆" hole, ¼"–½" up
into bottom of boot

Mitten
Cut 4 from red felt

Snowman
Cut 1 from pine

Doorknob Santa

Glue Santa's face and felt hat to this wooden doorknob hanger for an inviting holiday door!

Design by June Fiechter

Materials

- 3⅛" x 9½" square-top wooden door hanger*
- White felt
- Dark red embossed felt*
- Slick fabric paints*: peach, almond
- 4" winter white curly doll hair*
- Fabric glue*
- 2 (⅞6") black cabochons*
- 1" white jingle bell*
- 20" piece blue 18-gauge wire*
- Pink powdered cosmetic blusher
- Cotton-tip swab

Door hanger from Lara's Crafts; Classic Impressions embossed felt from Kunin; fabric paint and glue from Duncan; doll hair from One & Only Creations; cabochons from The Beadery; jingle bell from Darice; and wire from Toner Plastics.

Project Note

Refer to pattern and photo throughout.

Instructions

1. Find center of wire without bending it; match to center of door hanger's top edge, and glue wire along top edge of door hanger, leaving ends of wire unglued. Let glue dry.

2. *Face:* Glue cabochons in place for eyes, positioning them 3½" above bottom edge of door hanger. Add cheeks by rubbing two circles of pink cosmetic blusher onto door hanger with cotton-tipped swab. For nose, apply a blob of peach paint a little smaller than a dime just below eyes; bottoms of eyes should touch top of nose.

3. *Beard, mustache and eyebrows:* From white felt, cut one piece 3½"

W x 3" H; along top (3") edge, cut two "humps" to form top curves of mustache. Glue to bottom of door hanger below face, with bottom of felt even with edge of door hanger; carefully trim any excess felt from sides and bottom. Cut eyebrows from white felt; glue above eyes. Outline and add detail lines to eyebrows, mustache and beard with almond paint; add mouth with a small drop of peach paint.

4. *Hat:* From ruby embossed felt, cut two 4" W x 9" H pieces. Glue one piece to wrong side of door hanger so that bottom of felt is 5" below top edge of door hanger. Trim felt from door hanger's circular opening, leaving a margin of ½" felt to fold over edge. Cut slits in this margin; fold tabs of felt smoothly over edges of opening and glue in place on front of door hanger. Trim excess felt from sides of door hanger.

5. Fold free ends of wire attached in step 1 straight up. Glue second piece of felt onto front of door hanger as in step 4, trimming excess felt from circle and folding tabs to back of door hanger. *Do not* trim excess felt from sides, but fold it around edges of door hanger and glue on back.

6. *Backing:* From ruby embossed felt, cut a piece 3¼" W x 6" H; glue this piece of felt over felt on back of door hanger to cover raw edges, trimming out circle entirely (no margin) and trimming top of felt to match top edge of door hanger.

7. *Hat fringe:* Clipping straight down, fringe top edges of ruby felt hat, making cuts 1" long and ¼" apart.

8. Twist ends of wire together just below fringe to make a wire

triangular "armature" for hat. Poke wire ends out back at base of fringe, then wrap around top of felt hat, gathering top of hat closed and twisting wire into a bow on front of hat. Thread jingle bell onto wire at center of bow.

9. *Hair:* Glue curly hair above eyebrows to cover bottom edge of hat. ❄

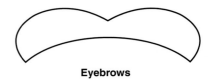

Eyebrows

Christmas Light Elves

Toss this pillow featuring decorating elves on a couch or bed to liven up any room with the Christmas spirit.

Design by Barbara Woolley

Materials

- 2 Christmas plaid or print napkins
- 18" pillow form
- 2¼ yards 2"-wide dark green fringe
- ½ yard fusible web*
- Felt: green, red, flesh tone, purple, light blue, yellow, pink, goldenrod, black
- Scraps of Christmasy fabric
- Pinking shears (optional)
- 1½ yards black satin rat-tail cording
- 4 (½") red buttons
- 2 (½") red metallic pompoms
- 2 (1") bows tied from ¼" white satin ribbon
- Scraps of red curly doll hair
- Fabric glue
- White thread and hand-sewing needle
- Black fine-point marker or fabric pen
- Pink fabric paint
- Small paintbrush

Steam-A-Seam 2 fusible web from The Warm Company.

Project Notes

Refer to patterns on this page and page 65 and photo throughout. Dashed lines indicate portions covered by other pieces.

Follow manufacturer's instructions for using fusible web.

Instructions

1. Launder and dry napkins without using fabric softener; press as needed to remove wrinkles.

2. Cut felt pieces according to patterns.

3. Cut matching pieces from fusible web for all pieces cut in step 2 *except* hat brims; fuse to backs of felt and fabric pieces. Trim bottom edge of jackets with pinking shears if desired.

4. Fuse elves' jackets, hats, leggings and shoes in place on one of the napkins. Fuse faces to elves, adding glue as needed; add facial features with black marker and blush cheeks with pink paint; let dry.

5. Position a few strands of doll hair on elves' heads and glue hat brims over them so that a few curls protrude from under brims.

6. Using needle and thread, sew bow at each elf's neckline; sew two buttons, evenly spaced, down front of each jacket. Glue pompom to tip of each elf's hat.

7. Using fabric glue, glue rat-tail cord to napkin for electrical cord, coiling it around as shown; at same time, fuse elves' mittens in place, under and over cord, so that they appear to be holding string of lights. Fuse socket and plug to ends of light string; fuse light bulbs along string, leaving room to attach black sockets so that they overlap broad ends of light bulbs and light string.

8. Lay decorated pillow top right side up; lay fringe around edge, pinning as needed, with fringe pointing toward center of pillow. Top with remaining napkin (pillow back), right side down. Pin layers together as needed and sew all layers together around three sides, leaving an opening in fourth side large enough to insert pillow form.

9. Turn pillow right side out. Insert form in open side; hand-stitch opening closed. ❁

JOY
For Spoon Elf cut 1 of each letter from red felt and 1 of each from green felt
For Christmas Light Elves cut 1 of each from red felt

Spoon Elf

Turn an ordinary wooden spoon into one of Santa's little helpers with scraps of brightly colored felt!

Design by Barbara Woolley

Materials
- ¼ yard fusible web*
- 15" wooden spoon
- Christmas green glossy spray paint
- Felt squares: green, red, flesh tone
- ½" green metallic pompom
- Scraps of Christmasy fabric
- Pinking shears (optional)
- 1 yard red satin rat-tail cording
- 3 (½") red buttons
- 1" bow tied from ¼"-wide white satin ribbon
- Scrap of red curly doll hair
- Fabric glue
- White thread and hand-sewing needle
- Black fine-point marker or fabric pen
- Pink fabric paint
- Small paintbrush

Steam-A-Seam 2 fusible web from The Warm Company.

Project Notes

Refer to patterns on pages 62, 64 and 65 and photo throughout.

Follow manufacturer's instructions for using fusible web.

Instructions

1. Spray wooden spoon with green spray paint; let dry.

2. Trace a complete elf outline and one of each letter onto fusible web; fuse elf pattern to red felt and letter patterns to green felt, and cut out.

3. Cut one of each letter from red felt; remove backing from fusible web and fuse red letters to green ones. Cut mittens from red felt, elf's shoes and jacket from green felt, and leggings and hat from fabric; trim bottom edge of jacket with pinking shears if desired. Remove backing from fusible web and fuse jacket, mittens, hat, leggings and shoes in place.

4. Cut face from flesh-tone felt and hat brim from red. Fuse face to elf, adding glue as needed; add facial features with black marker and blush cheeks with pink paint; let dry.

5. Position a few strands of doll hair on elf's head and glue hat brim over them so that a few curls protrude from under brim.

6. Using needle and thread, sew bow to elf's neckline and sew buttons, evenly spaced, down front of jacket. Glue pompom to tip of hat.

7. Glue wrong sides of tops of letters to front of spoon; glue fronts of elf's hands to back of spoon and back of hat to front of spoon.

8. *Hanger:* Wrap ends of rat-tail cord around spoon handle at end and next to bowl of spoon; secure with glue. ❈

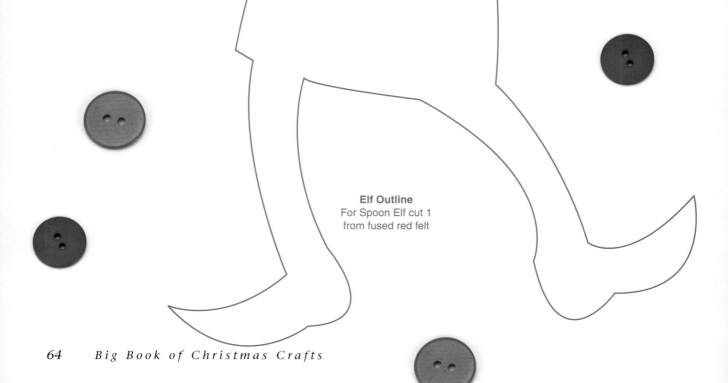

Elf Outline
For Spoon Elf cut 1
from fused red felt

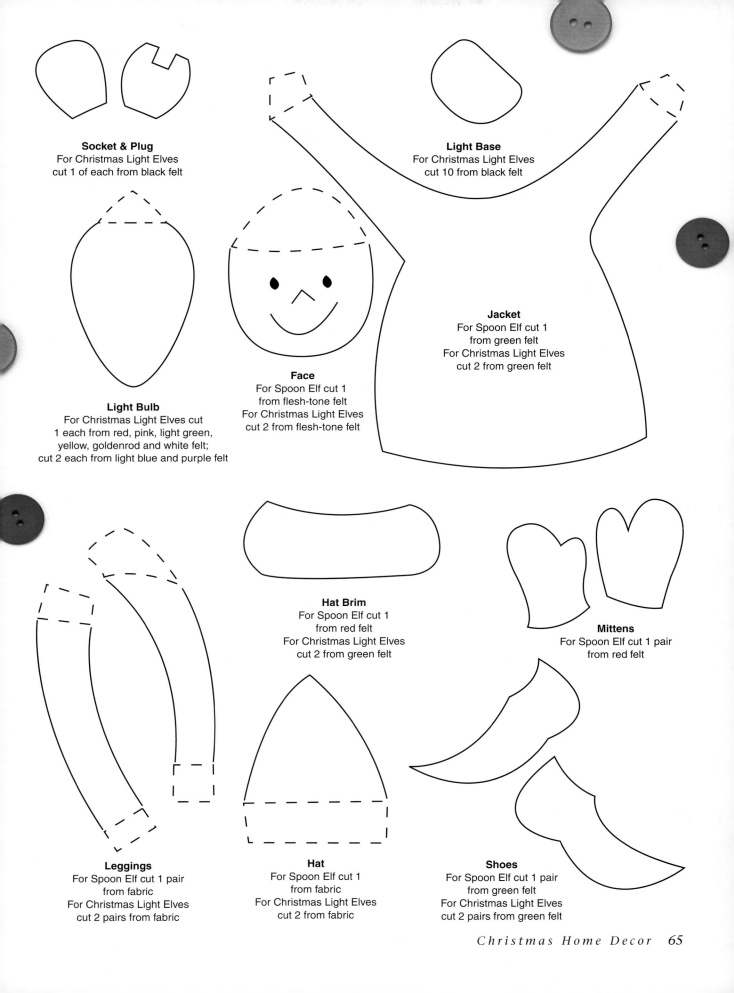

Socket & Plug
For Christmas Light Elves
cut 1 of each from black felt

Light Base
For Christmas Light Elves
cut 10 from black felt

Light Bulb
For Christmas Light Elves cut
1 each from red, pink, light green,
yellow, goldenrod and white felt;
cut 2 each from light blue and purple felt

Face
For Spoon Elf cut 1
from flesh-tone felt
For Christmas Light Elves
cut 2 from flesh-tone felt

Jacket
For Spoon Elf cut 1
from green felt
For Christmas Light Elves
cut 2 from green felt

Hat Brim
For Spoon Elf cut 1
from red felt
For Christmas Light Elves
cut 2 from green felt

Mittens
For Spoon Elf cut 1 pair
from red felt

Leggings
For Spoon Elf cut 1 pair
from fabric
For Christmas Light Elves
cut 2 pairs from fabric

Hat
For Spoon Elf cut 1
from fabric
For Christmas Light Elves
cut 2 from fabric

Shoes
For Spoon Elf cut 1 pair
from green felt
For Christmas Light Elves
cut 2 pairs from green felt

Angel Bathroom Decor

Dress up the usually forgotten room of your home for the holidays.
This toothbrush caddy, towel and light switch plate will complete your holiday home.

Designs by Mary Cosgrove

Materials

- Single acrylic switch plate*
- Acrylic toothbrush caddy*
- Acrylic dispenser*
- Rubber stamps*: country angel, joy, star trio
- White velour fingertip towel with even-weave inset*
- Holiday stencils*: holly and peace, angels
- Joy monogram stencil*
- Gold glitter fabric color*
- Candle and soap painting medium*
- Gold acrylic paint
- Small nylon paintbrushes
- 5" gold towel ring*
- Personal-size bar Ivory soap
- 1 yard ¼"-wide white satin ribbon
- Uncoated white paper
- Rubbing alcohol
- Plastic knife

Acrylic bathroom accessories from Crafter's Pride; fingertip towel #VT-6995-6750 from Charles Craft; Country Angel #2789D, JOY #A2622B and Star Trio #A1055C from Rubber Stampede; Holiday Stencils Holly and Peace #88-085-0310 and Angels #88-082-0310, Monogram Magic Sentiments Joy #88-062-0310, Starlite Glittering Fabric Color, Ceramcoat Candle & Soap Painting Medium, and Gleams acrylic paint from Delta; and towel ring from Uniek.

Project Note

Refer to photo throughout.

Switch Plate, Toothbrush Caddy & Dispenser

1. Using inserts accompanying switch plate, toothbrush caddy and dispenser as templates, cut pieces of white paper to fit inside acrylic pieces.

2. Using gold ink stamp pad, stamp paper inserts:

Switch plate: Stamp angel at top and bottom; add star trio and Joy on each side, alternating positions.

Toothbrush caddy: At right end of paper strip, stamp angel in center with Joy above and below it; to left of angel, stamp two star trios, one on top half of paper and the other on bottom half; to left of stars, repeat angel/Joy pattern, and finally, a second pair of star trios.

Dispenser: Along center of strip, stamp star trio, angel, star trio, angel. Stamp Joy three times in top margin, spacing them evenly; repeat in bottom margin.

3. Let inks dry thoroughly before placing paper inserts inside acrylic accessories.

Towel

1. Using small paintbrush and gold glitter fabric color, stencil only the J, O and Y from monogram stencils across even-weave area.

2. On each side of "JOY," stencil two small angels with stars from holiday angels stencils.

3. Stencil a large star from holiday holly and peace stencil between J and O, and between O and Y; stencil another large star above the area between the two angels on one end, and another large star below the same area. Repeat on other end of towel.

4. Cut ribbon in half. Holding pieces together, tie in a bow around center top of gold ring. Hang towel on bottom of ring.

Soap

1. Using plastic knife, scrape lettering from soap and smooth surface; clean surface with alcohol and let dry.

2. Mix equal parts candle and soap painting medium and gold acrylic paint. On top half of bar, stencil two angels with stars from holiday angels stencil. On bottom half of bar, stencil "Joy" with two stars on either side from holly and peace stencil.

3. When paints are dry, coat with candle and soap painting medium. ❉

Snowman Gel Candle

Inside this snowman hides a colorful candle of cubed gel!
Once melted, the gel can be cooled and burned again.

Design by Nicholas Tittle for Delta Technical Coatings

Materials

- Tuna cans, clean and dry, labels removed: 2 small, 1 medium
- Gesso
- Decorative snow
- Palette knife
- Acrylic paints*: white, black
- Sparkle glaze*
- Paintbrushes: #8 shader, #3 round
- Orange modeling compound or clay
- 2 (7⁄16") flat dark blue buttons
- 3 small black coffee-bean beads
- 2" red embroidery floss
- Kreative Kanvas coaster*
- Recycled compact disk
- 4" artificial fir pick
- Small pinecone
- Raffia: 6" each natural and red
- Garnet and emerald gel candle tubs*
- Tacky glue*

Decorative Tub O Snow, Ceramcoat acrylic paints, Sparkle Glaze, Gel Candle Tubs and Quick n Tacky Glue from Delta; and coaster from Kunin.

Project Notes

Refer to photo throughout.

Let gesso, snow, paint and sparkle glaze dry between applications.

Follow manufacturer's instructions for working with modeling compound or clay.

Instructions

1. Make a 1" orange carrot nose from orange modeling compound or clay; bake or dry as directed.

2. Remove top from each can. Paint exteriors of cans with gesso.

3. Set larger can (snowman's body) bottom up; using palette knife, cover can with decorative snow. Cover sides only of one smaller can (snowman's head) with snow and set can closed end down on top of larger can, pushing smaller can into snow.

4. *Face and buttons:* While snow is still wet, push flat buttons into snow on smaller can for eyes and coffee-bean beads into snow on larger can for buttons. Glue base of carrot nose between eyes, and glue red embroidery floss to head for smile. Let dry.

5. *Hat:* Paint remaining can and printed side of CD with black paint. Glue can, open end down, onto center of CD's black surface. Paint hat with Sparkle Glaze.

6. *Hat decoration:* Mix a small amount of white paint with an equal amount of water. Spatter fir pick with mixture. Hold natural and red raffia together and tie in a simple bow. Glue pinecone to fir pick and raffia bow to pinecone. Glue fir pick to brim of hat.

7. Glue coaster onto bottom of snowman.

8. *Candle:* Cut equal amounts of both colors of gel candle into small cubes. Set wick's disk in bottom of can (snowman's head); surround with cubed gel candle, pressing it down firmly. Place hat on top of snowman's head. ❄

Frosty Etched Mirror

Turn a plain mirror into a Christmas masterpiece with a festive rub-on!

Design by Marlene Watson

Materials

- 8" x 10" mirror framed in silver- or pewter-finish frame
- Rub-on Christmas tree*
- Window cleaner
- Lint-free cloth or paper towel
- Wooden craft stick

Frosty Etch Christmas tree #FE001FLG from ChartPak.

Project Note

Refer to manufacturer's instructions for using rub-on transfer.

Instructions

1. Remove mirror from frame. Clean mirror with window cleaner and lint-free cloth or paper towel; dry thoroughly.

2. Leaving backing tissue in place, cut out design, being sure to trim off labeling at bottom of transfer.

3. Remove tissue backing; carefully position design face-up on mirror; design will stick where it is placed.

4. Lift one corner slightly with index finger. Using craft stick, gently rub toward lifting finger.

Work your way across the design until carrier sheet is released; discard carrier sheet.

5. Wipe tissue backing over design to smooth it perfectly to the surface.

6. Replace mirror in frame. ❊

Holiday Floor Cloth

Create a dazzling holiday home accent with a ready-made floor cloth and paints in vibrant Christmas colors.

Design by Shelia Sommers

Materials

- 35" x 28" oval floor cloth*
- Acrylic paints*: green isle, cardinal red, burnt umber, raw sienna, fuchsia, eggplant, phthalo green, purple smoke, magenta, fuchsia pearl
- Metallic acrylic paints*: silver, 14K gold
- Glitter fabric color*
- Textile medium*
- Gloss exterior varnish
- Fabric paintbrushes: ¾" wash, ¼" and ⅜" angulars, #4 and #8 flats, 5/0 liner
- Fine-tip black permanent pen*
- Gray and white graphite papers
- Stylus

Floor cloth from Kunin; Ceramcoat acrylic paints, fabric color and textile medium from Delta; and .01 black pen from Sakura.

Project Notes

Refer to photo and patterns (page 72) throughout.

To transfer patterns, refer to instructions for "Using Transfer & Graphite Paper" in the General Instructions, page 190.

Refer to directions for base-coating and shading under "Paint Techniques" in General Instructions, page 190.

Instructions

1. Using a pencil, draw an oval in the center of the floor cloth leaving a 4½"-wide border on the outside. Paint oval with sufficient coats of cardinal to produce an opaque shade of color, adding additional layers while paint is still wet.

2. Draw a second oval ¼" from edge of floor cloth. Using liner, paint line cardinal, staying up on the tip of the brush.

3. Using #4 flat brush, paint a ⅜"-wide gold stripe around edge of red oval.

4. Trace and transfer line work for the holiday designs randomly around outer band of floor cloth between thin red line and gold stripe, making sure no portion of any design overlaps red line or gold band.

5. Paint designs:

Gingerbread men: Base-coat with raw sienna; shade with burnt umber. Thin a little fuchsia pearl with enough textile medium to produce a transparent shade of color and add cheeks to face with mixture. Using black, add ovals for eyes, eyelashes and mouth. Using shading technique, add burnt umber nose between eyes. Using liner, outline each section of gingerbread man with thin wavy line of white. Add buttons to tummies using end of paintbrush handle dipped in silver.

Peppermint sticks and candies: The white of the floor cloth serves as the base color for these pieces. Paint cardinal stripes on both sticks & candies. On candies, add a thin stripe of green isle on one side of red stripes; on sticks, add two thin stripes of green isle on one side of red stripes. Blend a little purple smoke with enough textile medium to produce a transparent shade and shade candies and sticks with mixture.

Wrapped candies: Base-coat wrappers with gold; shade with raw sienna. Paint end of candy fuchsia; shade with eggplant. Using liner and gold, add several short, thin lines in center of fuchsia circle and middle of opposite end.

Holly leaves: Base-coat with green isle; shade with phthalo green, adding veins with liner. Add fuchsia highlight to each leaf tip.

Holly berries: Using end of brush handle dipped in cardinal, add large dots; shade with eggplant, adding a tiny fuchsia highlight dot.

Ornaments: Base-coat with cardinal; shade with eggplant, adding crystal ice to opposite side. Paint top of ornament cap silver.

6. Using black pen, lightly outline peppermint stick and peppermint candies, adding ¾" circle to top of cap on ornament for hanging loop.

7. Allow all paints to dry before applying several heavy coats of gloss exterior varnish to front and back of floor cloth. ❊

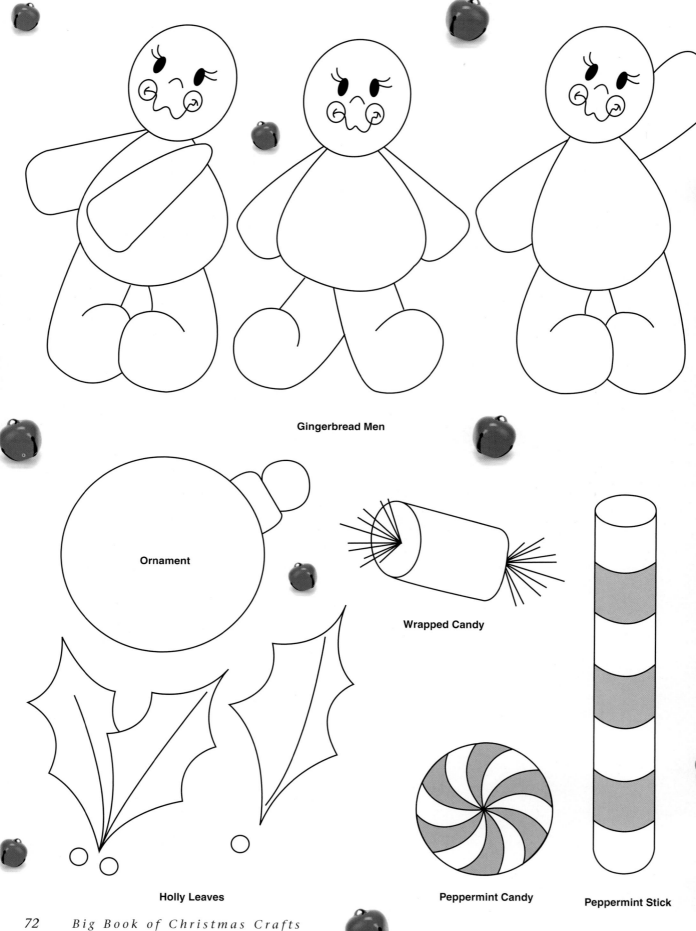

Gingerbread Men

Ornament

Wrapped Candy

Holly Leaves

Peppermint Candy

Peppermint Stick

Christmas Apple Wreath

One of Christmas' staples is a rich and beautiful wreath. Add a big plaid bow to this wreath, decorated with apples, piñon cones, eucalyptus and pheasant feathers for a lovely addition to your home.

Design by Charlene Messerle

Materials

- 24" green pine wreath
- Artificial apples: 10 (2½"), 12 (1½"), 6 (1¼")
- 12–15 piñon cones
- Green eucalyptus leaves
- 7 pheasant feathers
- 3 yards 2⅝"-wide red plaid gold-edged wire ribbon*
- Thin craft wire
- Matte spray varnish*

Lion MW Milton ribbon and matte spray varnish from Krylon.

Continued on page 86

Noel Garland

Hang this holiday greeting from a doorway, or drape across a wall to add holiday cheer to your home!

Design by Mary Ayres

Materials

- Light blue sparkle paper
- Parchment white translucent vellum*
- Medium blue card stock
- Coordinating blue decorative papers: 4 light patterns and 1 dark
- 14 (8mm) clear pearl sequins
- Writers*: blue fine-tip permanent, opaque white extra-fine-tip
- 2-way glue*
- Pinking paper edgers*
- White cord
- 10 miniature spring clothespins

Vellum from Glama Natural; ZIG Memory System writers and 2-Way Glue from EK Success Ltd.; and paper edgers from Fiskars.

Project Notes

Refer to patterns and photo throughout.

Use regular scissors for cutting unless instructed otherwise.

Letters

1. Following inner lines, cut each letter from a different light blue paper. Using blue writer, draw "stitching lines" around edges of letters.

2. Following outer lines and using edgers, cut a medium blue card stock background piece for each letter. Using white writer, draw buttonhole stitches around outer edges with lines pointed outward between "pinking" points. Glue letters onto background shapes.

3. Following inner lines and using

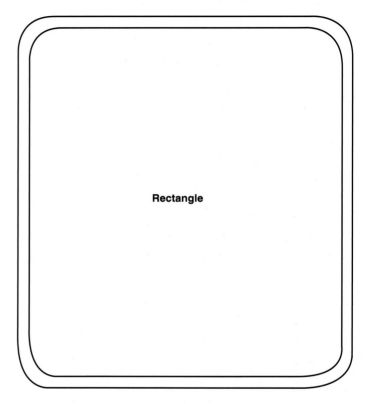

Rectangle

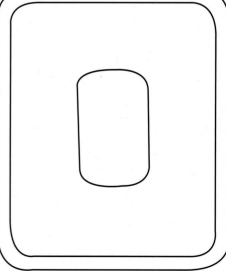

edgers, cut four smaller rectangles from vellum. Using blue writer, draw buttonhole stitches around outer edges with lines pointed

outward between "pinking" points. Glue assembled letter shapes to vellum rectangles.

Continued on page 78

Snowflake

Stitcher's Mini Tree

Boughs laden with colorful spools of thread and mini "tomato" pincushions, this is just the thing to decorate your sewing room for the holidays!

Design by Chris Malone

Materials

- 15" miniature Christmas tree on wooden stand
- Felt*: 1 sheet each red and antique white; ½ sheet each pirate green and apple green; small piece gold
- 9 (1") plastic foam balls
- 12 (¾" x ⅝") wooden spools
- 2¾" brass scissors charm
- ½" brass thimble button, shank removed
- Flat buttons: ½" black; 26 (⅜"–1") assorted bright colors
- Grosgrain ribbon: 3 yards ¼"-wide yellow, 12" ⅜"-wide red
- Assorted bright colors of pearl cotton or embroidery floss
- 45 straight pins with multicolored plastic heads
- 6-strand embroidery floss: black, bright green
- Quilting or buttonhole thread
- Embroidery and sewing needles
- Craft glue
- Hot-glue gun
- Toothpick

Felt from Kunin.

Project Notes

Refer to patterns and photo throughout.

Use 2 strands floss for all buttonhole stitch, fly stitch and running stitch.

Instructions

1. Fold antique white felt in half; cut one tree skirt on fold. Cut two stars from gold, 33 leaves from apple green, nine pincushion caps from pirate green and nine pincushions from red.

2. Cut straight through tree skirt from outer edge to center opening. Blanket-stitch around all edges of tree skirt.

3. Lay tree skirt flat on work surface. Arrange three groups of five button "flowers" and five leaves each around skirt. **Note:** *Reserve nine larger buttons for tree.* Center one group at front (opposite slit cut in step 2) and position other groups between center group and back opening. Using 2 strands black floss, sew buttons in place and attach each leaf by sewing two fly stitches down its center.

4. Cut red ribbon in half; tack one end of each piece at top back opening. Sew small button on top of ribbon end. Wrap skirt around base of tree and tie ribbons in a bow at back.

5. *Button flowers for tree:* Using black floss, sew two fly stitches in each remaining leaf as for tree skirt. Glue broad ends of two leaves behind each of nine reserved buttons.

6. *Spools:* Using toothpick, spread a light coat of craft glue over center section of each spool. Wrap neatly with pearl cotton or embroidery floss in a variety of colors to cover center area smoothly and completely.

7. *Pincushions:* Sew gathering stitch around edge of red felt circle using quilting or buttonhole thread. Place plastic foam ball in center of felt and gather felt around it; knot and clip thread. Using 2 strands green floss, take a small stitch through gathers at top of ball, then wrap around ball to divide pincushion in half; take a stitch and wrap floss in other direction to divide pincushion into quarters. Bring threaded needle up through center of green felt pincushion cap; push cap down onto top of ball and make one straight stitch down each leaf. Repeat to make a total of nine pincushions. Partially insert five straight pins in each pincushion, dipping tips of pin lightly in craft glue before inserting them.

8. *Star:* Using black floss, sew stars together with running stitch. Sew ½" black button in center of star.

9. *Decorating tree:* Glue star to top of tree. Glue brass thimble to front of scissors; glue scissors to top of tree under star. Cut yellow ribbon into 12 (8") lengths. Thread one through center hole of each spool; tie spools to boughs of tree, tying ribbon ends in bows. Glue pincushions and button flowers to tree boughs. ❁

Pincushion Cap
Cut 9 from pirate green

Leaf
Cut 33 from apple green

Patterns continued on page 78

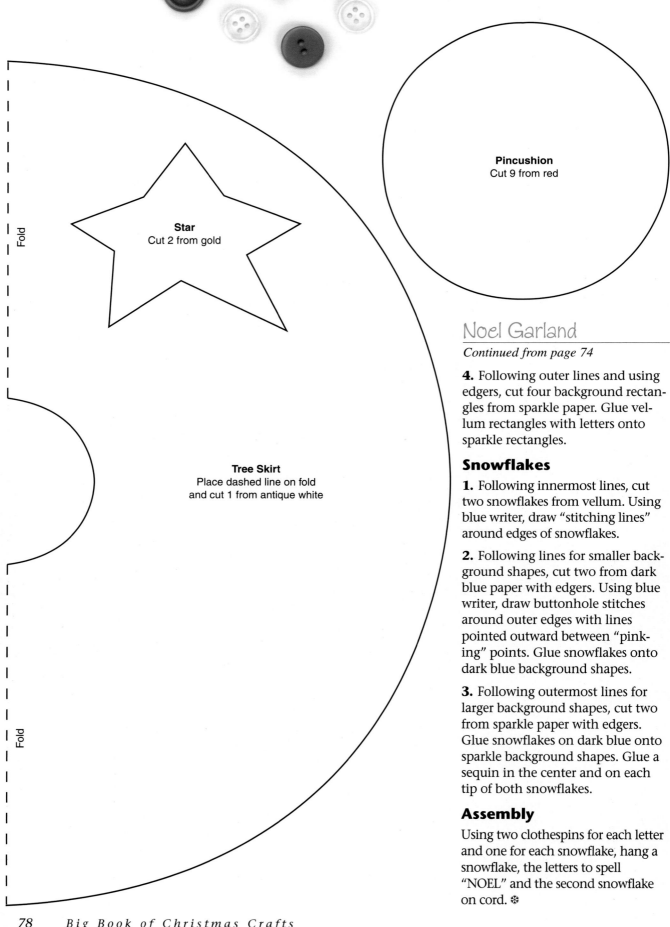

Pincushion
Cut 9 from red

Star
Cut 2 from gold

Tree Skirt
Place dashed line on fold
and cut 1 from antique white

Fold

Fold

Noel Garland

Continued from page 74

4. Following outer lines and using edgers, cut four background rectangles from sparkle paper. Glue vellum rectangles with letters onto sparkle rectangles.

Snowflakes

1. Following innermost lines, cut two snowflakes from vellum. Using blue writer, draw "stitching lines" around edges of snowflakes.

2. Following lines for smaller background shapes, cut two from dark blue paper with edgers. Using blue writer, draw buttonhole stitches around outer edges with lines pointed outward between "pinking" points. Glue snowflakes onto dark blue background shapes.

3. Following outermost lines for larger background shapes, cut two from sparkle paper with edgers. Glue snowflakes on dark blue onto sparkle background shapes. Glue a sequin in the center and on each tip of both snowflakes.

Assembly

Using two clothespins for each letter and one for each snowflake, hang a snowflake, the letters to spell "NOEL" and the second snowflake on cord. ✻

Snowed Inn Birdhouse

Welcome snowbirds one and all into this cozy, crafted inn!

Design by June Fiechter

Materials

- Wood: 12" x 3¼" x 1½" piece lumber, 2 (2" x 3¾") ¼"-thick slats, 1" x 2½" ¼"-thick rectangle
- 3 (2¼"-long) ¼" wooden dowels
- Oak wood stain*
- Wood glue
- 36" natural dried grapevine
- 2 small wood screws and screwdriver
- Artificial/silk botanicals: 7 artificial blue berries, 6 green silk leaves, small sprigs of coordinating dried flowers or tiny berries for filler
- Dried Spanish moss
- 6" black 24-gauge wire*
- Foam glue*
- 3 (¾") red "mushroom" birds
- Decorative snow*
- White acrylic paint
- Small paintbrush
- Toothbrush
- Fine-point black permanent marker
- Craft saw
- Drill with ¹⁄₁₆", ⅛", ¼" and 1" bits

Aleene's oil-based Wood Stain, Foamtastic Glue, and decorative Snow from Duncan; and wire from Toner Plastics.

Project Notes

Refer to photo throughout.

Refer to manufacturer's instructions for applying wood stain.

Instructions

1. Form peaked top on birdhouse by sawing two triangular pieces off top corners of 12" x 3¼" lumber, starting at center and sawing diagonally to a point 2" down side.

2. Drill three 1" holes for birdhouse openings evenly spaced down front of birdhouse; ¾" below each, drill a ¼" hole to accept perch (dowel) later.

3. Stain birdhouse, dowels and 2" x 3¾" slats with wood stain; let dry.

4. Using wood glue, glue stained slats to top of birdhouse for roof and dowels in ¼" holes.

5. Lightly spatter birdhouse using toothbrush and white paint; let dry.

6. Wrap vine around birdhouse as desired; hold vine in place by drilling with ¹⁄₁₆" bit through ends of vine into birdhouse, and securing ends with small wood screws.

7. Using foam glue throughout, glue berries and leaves to roof and birdhouse base and sides; add bits of dried Spanish moss and filler as desired.

8. Glue a bird in each large opening, adding a few sprigs of Spanish moss for "nests."

9. Apply snow to roof, perches, openings, vine and leaves and berries as desired; let dry.

Sign

1. Paint 1" x 2½" wooden rectangle white; let dry. Drill a ⅛" hole in each upper corner.

2. Using black marker, write "SNOWED INN" on sign and add snowflake decoration to sign as desired.

3. Thread wire ends through holes in sign; twist ends to secure. Hang sign from birdhouse perch. ✻

Sugarplum Twinklers

Paint these fairies dropping sweet gifts on your lamp shade for a warm glow during the holiday season!

Design by Annie Lang

Materials

- Miniature white lamp shade: 4" tall, 5" diameter at bottom, 2½" diameter at top
- Matte spray*
- Acrylic paints*: white, buttermilk, baby pink, baby blue, mint julep green, mistletoe, cranberry wine, French vanilla, soft peach
- Clear glitter paint*
- Paintbrushes: #4 and #6 shaders, ¼" and ⅛" angle shaders, #3 and #8 pointed rounds, #2 and #0 liners
- Decorative snow*
- Palette knife
- Black extra-fine-line marking pen
- Graphite paper

Americana matte spray and acrylic paints, Craft Twinkles clear glitter paint and decorative snow from DecoArt.

Project Notes

Refer to photo and pattern throughout.

Use photocopier to enlarge pattern 140 percent before transferring.

To transfer pattern, refer to directions for "Using Transfer & Graphite Paper" in General Instructions, page 190.

Refer to directions for base-coating, shading and floating under "Painting Techniques" in General Instructions, page 190.

Allow all coats of matte spray, paints and decorative snow to dry between applications.

Preparation

1. Spray lamp shade with two or three coats of matte spray. (Transferred and final ink lines tend to bleed on lamp shade surfaces; this step is recommended to avoid that problem.)

2. Transfer design onto lamp shade, taping pattern and graphite paper in place on shade as necessary.

Painting

1. *Shading:* Thin baby blue with water to make a light wash; apply mixture to lamp shade as a shadowing color, just to the right of each motif.

2. *Round candies:* Paint inner area of circles with white; paint outer area of center circle pink. Mix a little cranberry with pink and shade side edges of candies with

Sugarplum Twinklers
Enlarge 140% before transferring

this mixture. Paint tree shapes in centers of candies with mistletoe.

3. *Gumdrops:* Paint gumdrops as desired with French vanilla, mint green and pink.

4. *Fairies:* Using flat brushes, paint gowns with buttermilk. Dampen ¼" angular brush with water and load one side with French vanilla; float this shading color around border edges of gowns and sleeves. Fill in shaded

bottom underskirt areas with French vanilla. Paint sashes mint green; shade with mistletoe. Base-coat wings with white; float edges with baby blue shading. Paint faces and hands peach; tap a tiny bit of cranberry onto cheeks. Paint hair French vanilla; paint wreaths in hair with mistletoe using #2 liner.

5. Outline and add details to designs with black marking pen.

Finishing

1. Apply clear glitter paint over dresses, wreaths in hair, wings and all candy.

2. Using flat brush, lightly glitter paint swirl onto white lamp shade around candy pieces.

3. Using palette knife, apply snow around top and bottom edges of lamp shade.

4. Brush snow with glitter paint. ❋

Snowman Tissue Topper

Stitch and glue this simple snowman design to camouflage your tissue boxes all around the house. This easy foam design works throughout the winter season.

Design by Barbara Matthiessen

Materials

- Craft foam: 2 sheets blue, 1 sheet white
- White craft foam flowers: 3 (1"), 8 (¾") (see Project Notes)
- 2 skeins white embroidery floss
- 3" x 12" strip plaid fabric
- Markers*: blue, orange and pink pigment markers, .05 permanent black marker
- Fabric adhesive*
- Craft knife
- Embroidery needle
- 1 or 2 small stencil brushes

ZIG markers from EK Success Ltd.; and Fabri-Tac adhesive from Beacon.

Project Notes

Refer to photo and patterns throughout.

Craft foam flowers are sold in bags of assorted sizes and colors; if desired, cut your own shapes from scraps of white craft foam.

Instructions

1. From blue craft foam cut four sides, 5" x 6", and one top, 5" square. Using a craft knife, cut 2" square opening in center of top. From white craft foam, cut two large and two small snowmen.

2. Using blue marker, shade foam

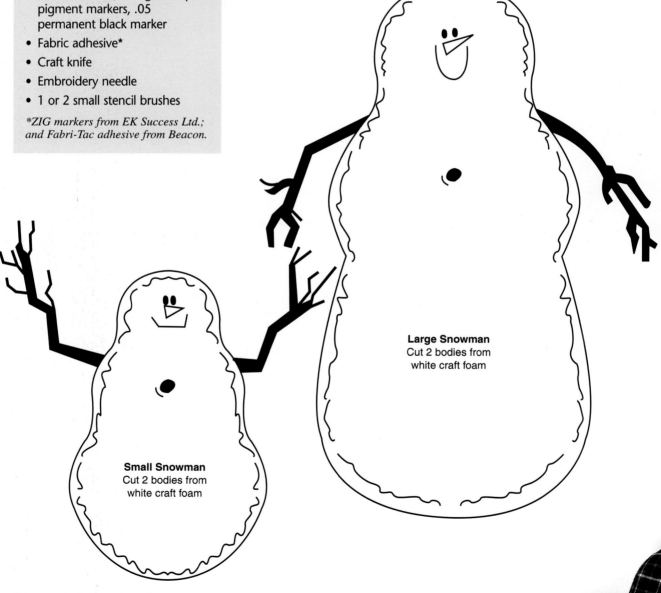

Large Snowman
Cut 2 bodies from white craft foam

Small Snowman
Cut 2 bodies from white craft foam

snowmen and flowers by running the wide (1.2mm) end around edges of foam, then stroking ink toward center with stencil brush.

3. Clean and dry the brush well, or switch to a different brush. Use brush to rub pink ink in circular motion to blush two cheeks on all snowmen.

4. Add noses to snowmen with orange marker. Using black marker throughout, add snowmen's eyes, buttons, smiles and outlines.

5. For snowflakes, add dots to white foam flowers, radiating out from center along each "petal."

6. From fabric tear two 1" x 8" strips and two ½" x 6" strips for snowmen's scarves. Tie larger strips around necks of larger snowmen and smaller strips around necks of smaller snowmen.

7. Using 6 strands white floss, join sides in a box shape with blanket stitch; blanket-stitch opening in top and blanket-stitch top to

assembled sides. Blanket-stitch bottom edges of tissue topper.

8. Glue large snowmen on opposite sides of tissue topper; glue small snowmen on remaining sides. Using black marker, draw snowmen's twig arms on blue background.

9. Glue a small snowflake in upper right corner on sides with larger snowmen. Glue one large and two small snowflakes to sides with smaller snowmen, and remaining snowflakes to top. ❄

Felt Banner Ornaments

These little holiday designs make wonderful tree trims and package ornaments.

Designs by Chris Malone

Materials

Snowman

- Felt*: 9" x 12" cadet blue, antique white, red, apple green, scrap of orange
- 6-strand embroidery floss*: ecru, black #310, Christmas red #321, medium cornflower blue #793, medium emerald green #911
- 2 slender 1½" twigs
- Ivory acrylic paint

Santa

- Felt*: 9" x 12" antique gold, antique white, red, apricot, antique white plush
- 6-strand embroidery floss*: ecru, black, red, dark gold
- ¼" wooden furniture button
- ⅜" brass jingle bell
- Acrylic paints: dark skin-tone, red

Each Project

- Small paintbrush
- 2 (2.5mm) black beads
- Wooden jumbo craft stick*
- 24" black 19-gauge craft wire
- Fabric adhesive*
- Satin-finish varnish
- Embroidery needle
- Craft drill with ⅙" bit

Felt from Kunin; embroidery floss from DMC; craft stick from Forster; and Fabri-Tac adhesive from Beacon.

Project Notes

Refer to photo and patterns throughout.

Use 2 strands embroidery floss for all stitching.

Allow all paints and varnish to dry thoroughly between coats.

Snowman

1. From cadet blue felt, cut 3¼" x 7" piece for banner front and 3¼" x 8½" piece for banner back. Cut snowman body from antique white felt, four mittens from apple green, carrot nose from orange, and scarf and additional ⅜" x 5½" strip from red.

2. Position snowman body on banner front with bottom of body 1" from bottom of banner front. Using blue floss, blanket-stitch around body. Attach scarf to snowman with red blanket stitch. Pin mittens together in pairs; join with green blanket stitch, leaving bottoms open.

3. Using black floss, sew beads to face for eyes. Straight-stitch eyebrows and mouth. Glue carrot nose to face.

4. Pin banner front and back together, wrong sides facing and bottom edges even. Using ecru floss and running stitch, stitch layers together, starting across top of short (front) piece, down the side and across bottom and up other side to top of long (back) piece. Fold top of back down 1¼" over front; stitch through all layers, finishing stitches at other side through one layer only.

5. Drill hole in craft stick ½" from each end. Paint stick ivory, using two coats if necessary. Finish with a coat of satin varnish.

6. Slip stick through casing at top of banner. Poke 2" of one end of wire through one of the holes in craft stick from back to front. Curl wire end around a pencil. Slip wire off pencil and push curls down on stick. Randomly curl remaining wire up to last 2" by wrapping it around pencil in various directions. Poke other end of wire through remaining hole and curl to hold hanger in place.

7. Apply glue to tip of one twig; slip inside one mitten and glue twig arm at snowman's side. Repeat with remaining twig and mitten.

8. Fringe red felt strip by making four ½" snips in each end. Tie knot in center of strip; glue knot over scarf at one side.

Santa

1. From antique gold felt, cut 3¼" x 7" piece for banner front and 3¼" x 8½" piece for banner back. Cut beard and four mustache pieces from antique white, hat from red, face from apricot and hat brim from plush felt.

2. Position beard, face and hat on banner front with bottom of beard 1" from bottom of banner front. Lightly glue face in place.

3. Using gold floss, blanket-stitch around beard; using red, blanket-stitch around hat. Blanket-stitch mustache pieces together in pairs with gold floss; glue mustache and hat brim in place.

4. Using black floss, sew beads to face for eyes. For nose, paint furniture button dark skin-tone; coat with satin varnish; glue to face.

5. Follow instructions in step 4 for snowman banner for joining banner front and back, substituting red floss for ecru.

6. For hanger, follow instructions in steps 5 and 6 for snowman banner, painting craft stick red instead of ivory. Sew jingle bell to tip of hat. ❋

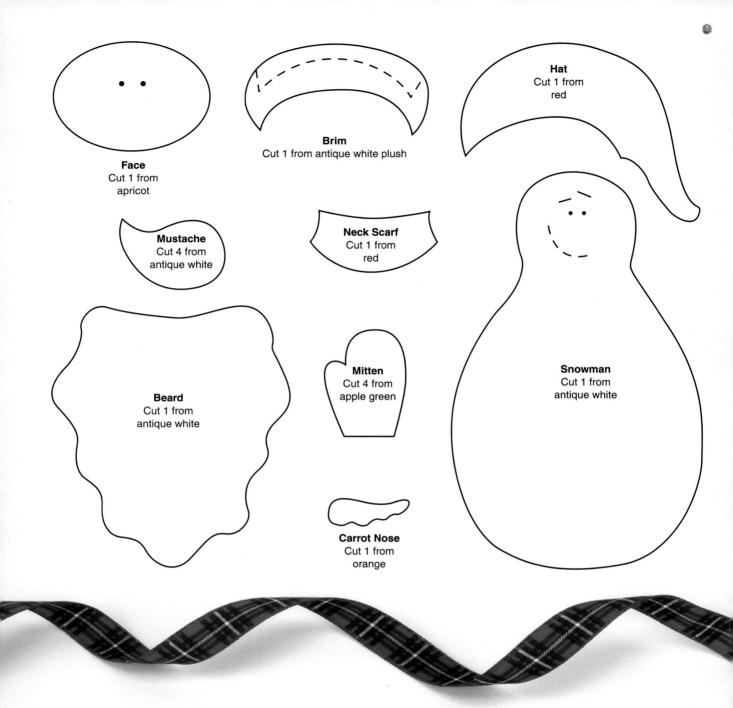

Face
Cut 1 from
apricot

Brim
Cut 1 from antique white plush

Hat
Cut 1 from
red

Mustache
Cut 4 from
antique white

Neck Scarf
Cut 1 from
red

Beard
Cut 1 from
antique white

Mitten
Cut 4 from
apple green

Snowman
Cut 1 from
antique white

Carrot Nose
Cut 1 from
orange

Christmas Apple Wreath

Continued from page 73

Project Note

Refer to photo throughout.

Instructions

1. Attach a hanging loop of thin wire to back of wreath.

2. *Bows:* Cut ribbon into one 1-yard piece and two ½-yard pieces. From each of the ½-yard pieces, make a 4" one-loop bow with two tails; secure with thin wire. From the 2-yard piece make a bow with four 4" loops and tails. Attach four-loop bow to wreath at bottom left; attach a one-loop bow to wreath on each side of larger bow.

3. Attach thin wires to each of the apples; attach to wreath randomly.

4. Attach wires to piñon cones; wire to wreath in a pleasing arrangement.

5. Break eucalyptus into 4"–6" pieces. Wire together in bunches of three pieces, making eight to 12 bunches total. Wire randomly onto wreath.

6. Attach wires to pheasant feathers. Wire feathers to wreath, breaking spines of feathers as needed to allow them to bend attractively.

7. Spray entire wreath with matte varnish to help hold the colors and preserve the eucalyptus. ❈

Sparkly Snowflakes

Make this sparkly winter rug from a simple bath mat, acrylic paints and some festive stamps!

Design by Barbara Matthiessen

Materials

- Blue 18" x 30" kitchen rug mat
- Rubber stamps*: jumbo snowflake, medallion
- Acrylic paints*: wicker white, true blue
- Iridescent blue sparkle paint*
- Cosmetic sponges
- Stiff paintbrush

Simply Stamps Jumbo Snowflake #19313, Stamp Decor Medallions #53662, FolkArt acrylic paints and Sparkles paint from Plaid.

Project Notes

Refer to photo throughout.

Follow manufacturer's instructions for using, cleaning and drying stamps.

Instructions

1. Place rug on a firm surface. Using a cosmetic sponge, apply a generous amount of blue paint to snowflake stamp, then press stamp very firmly onto rug, pressing down all edges. Repeat to stamp a total of six snowflakes randomly over rug.

2. In same manner and again using blue, stamp rug randomly with round stamp and four-point stamp from medallion stamp package. Let blue paint dry; clean stamps and dry thoroughly.

3. Repeat steps 1 and 2 using white paint and stamping off to one side so that the blue snowflakes and rounds appear to be shadows of the white ones. Also stamp a few four-point stamps by themselves, then turn the stamp a quarter-turn and stamp again in the same location. Allow paints to dry.

4. Using stiff brush, apply iridescent blue paint to centers of all white snowflakes, then out the arms of the jumbo snowflakes. Load brush with iridescent blue paint and randomly dab surface of rug.

5. Allow paints to dry for at least 48 hours before using rug and at least 72 hours before washing it. ❈

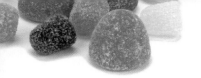

"Let It Snow!"

Paint this snowman picture for the look of stained glass to display on a table or shelf.

Design by June Fiechter

Materials
- Window colors*: white pearl, ivory, yellow, magenta, amber, lime green, sapphire, black
- Crackle medium*
- 7½" square free-standing wooden frame with no easel (opening at top or bottom)
- Leading strips*
- Styrene blank*
- Laser stencils*
- Paintbrushes: stencil brush, #10 flat
- Acrylic paints*: berry wine, wicker white
- Satin varnish*
- Toothpick
- Transparent tape

Gallery Glass window colors, crackle medium, Redi-Lead Lines #16092, styrene blank #16052, Simply Laser stencils #28036, FolkArt acrylic paints and satin varnish all from Plaid.

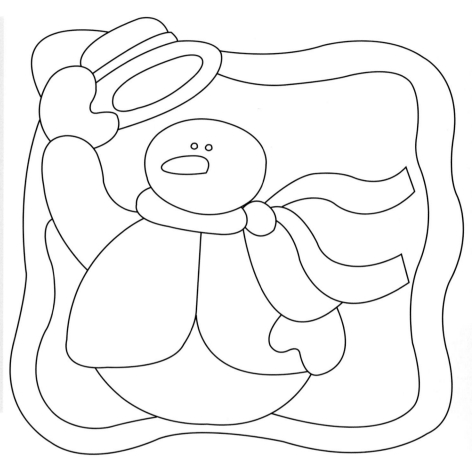

Project Notes

Refer to photo and pattern throughout.

Refer to manufacturer's directions for using window colors, leading, stencils, crackle medium and other products. Use the point of a toothpick to gently correct leading and pop bubbles in window colors.

Let all coats of paint and varnish dry between applications.

Instructions

1. Cut styrene blank to fit frame. Place pattern under styrene and tape it in position.

2. Apply leading strips onto styrene blank over pattern lines to complete outlines of picture.

3. Use window colors to paint design: *sapphire:* squarish background immediately behind snowman; *amber:* wavy border around sapphire background and snowman's nose; *ivory:* background outside amber border; *white pearl:* snowman's head and body; *magenta:* coat; *yellow:* scarf and hatband; *lime green:* mittens; *black:* hat. Pop bubbles in paints with point of toothpick. Let colors dry completely before moving.

4. Using flat brush, paint frame wine.

5. Using stencil brush and white paint, stencil "LET IT SNOW" on front edges of each of the frame's four sides. Wipe most of paint from brush and use it to stipple frame to depict snow.

6. Apply crackle medium only to ivory background; let dry completely.

7. Paint frame with varnish. When dry, insert styrene blank with snowman picture into frame. ❄

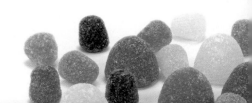

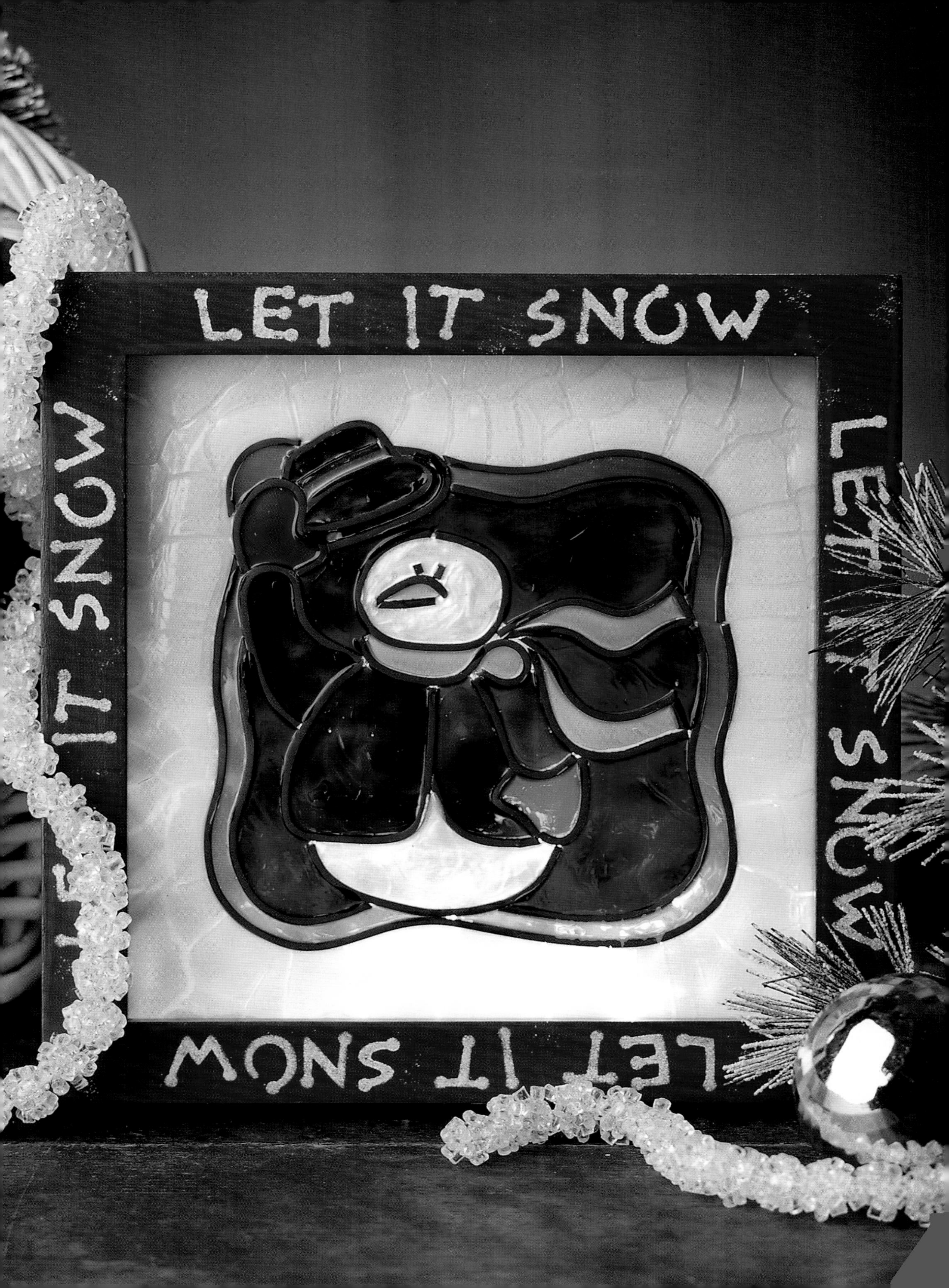
LET IT SNOW
LET IT SNOW
LET IT SNOW
LET IT SNOW

Tree Trims & Ornaments

Trimming the tree is more fun than ever when you decorate it with tiny ornaments and trims created by your own crafting hands! Sweet angels, mischievous elves, Americana Santas, sparkling icicles and many more festive ornaments are at your fingertips!

Geometric Wooden Ornaments

Turn simple wooden shapes into classic Christmas symbols with a little paint and a lot of fun!

Designs by Mary Ayres

Materials

All Ornaments

- Wooden cutouts*: 5 (1½")
  squares, ⅞" square, 4 (½")
  squares, 4 (1½" x 2") triangles, 2
  (1") stars, 3 (1½") hearts, 1" heart
- 5 (10") pieces metallic gold
  pearl cotton or fine cord
- Acrylic paints*: white wash,
  pumpkin, country blue, bright
  green, mocha, lamp black,
  sapphire, true red, honey
  brown, primary yellow
- Paintbrushes: #5 and #8 natural
  bristle brushes
- Glue*
- Twin-tip black permanent
  marker*
- Craft drill and 3⁄32" bit
- Scrap wood

*Woodsies wooden cutouts from
Forster; Americana acrylic paints
from DecoArt; Kids Choice Glue
from Beacon; and ZIG Memory
System marker from EK Success Ltd.*

Project Notes

Refer to photo and patterns
throughout.

Paint all surfaces of wooden
cutouts.

See directions for dry-brushing
and rouging under "Painting
Techniques" in the General
Instructions, page 190.

Let all paints and glue dry between
applications.

Instructions

1. Drill hole in cutouts where
indicated by X's on patterns,
laying cutouts on a piece of scrap
wood before drilling to keep them
from splitting:

Santa and *snowman:* stars; *reindeer*
and *penguin:* one 1½" square for
each; *polar bear:* 1½" heart.

2. Paint wooden cutouts:

Santa—mocha: 1½" square (face) and
½" square (nose); *white:* drilled star
and 1½" heart (beard/mustache);
red: one triangle (hat).

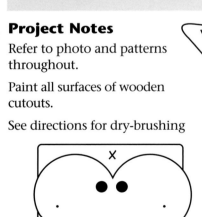

Penguin

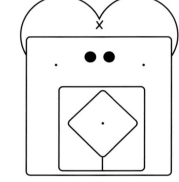

Polar Bear

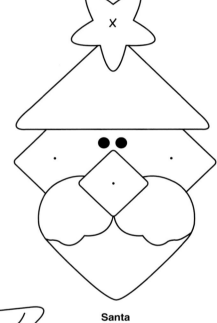

Santa

Reindeer

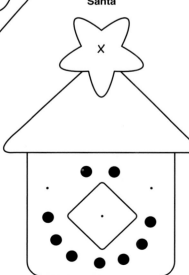

Snowman

Snowman—white: 1½" square (head); *pumpkin:* ½" square (nose); *green:* one triangle (hat); *blue:* drilled star.

Reindeer—brown: 1½" square (head); *red:* ½" square (nose); *blue:* two triangles (antlers).

Polar bear—white: drilled heart (ears), 1½" square (head) and ⅞" square (muzzle); *black:* ½" square (nose).

Penguin—white: 1½" heart (face); *yellow:* 1" heart (beak); *black:* drilled square (head).

3. Dry-brush edges of all painted pieces with sapphire.

4. Using red, rouge cheeks and nose on Santa and cheeks of all other characters. Using tip of paintbrush handle dipped in white, add highlight dots to cheeks and noses where indicated by tiny dots on patterns.

5. Using fine tip of marking pen, add details to ornaments:

Santa: mustache line on beard/mustache.

Reindeer: mouth on head and antler lines on triangles.

Polar bear: vertical line at bottom of muzzle.

Penguin: nostrils and mouth on beak.

6. Using bullet tip of marking pen, add eyes to all ornaments and mouth to snowman.

7. Glue wooden components together, taking care to position drilled holes correctly and making sure that all holes remain open.

8. Thread gold pearl cotton through hole in each ornament; knot ends together for hanging loop. ✻

Sleepy Puppy & Kitten

Paint these snoozing pets in stockings for a colorful addition to your tree!

Designs by Vicki Schreiner

Materials
Both Ornaments
- 8" square Baltic birch
- Clear glaze base*
- Satin interior varnish*
- Acrylic paints*: Dresden flesh, Georgia clay, tompte red, brown velvet, dusty mauve, Bridgeport grey, hydrangea pink, hunter green, barn red, white, eucalyptus
- Paintbrushes: #4 shader, #4 filbert, #3 round, #1 liner
- Black fine-point permanent marker*
- Black graphite paper
- 2 (7") pieces white or silver ¼"-wide ribbon
- Masking tape
- Scroll saw
- Craft drill with ⅛" bit
- Sandpaper

Ceramcoat clear glaze base, satin varnish and acrylic paints from Delta; and IdentiPen marker from Sakura.

Project Notes

Refer to photo and patterns throughout.

See directions for transferring pattern under "Using Transfer & Graphite Paper" in the General Instructions, page 190. Do not transfer stippling dots; these are for your reference when shading.

For all painting, mix paints with equal part glaze base.

See directions for base-coating under "Painting Techniques" in the General Instructions, page 190.

Carry painted designs over onto edges of ornaments; leave backs of ornaments unpainted or paint with a complementary background color as desired.

Let all applications of paints, ink and varnish dry between coats.

Preparation

1. Transfer outlines of patterns onto birch; cut out with scroll saw. Drill holes for hangers. Sand all surfaces and edges until smooth.

2. Transfer remainder of designs to wooden cutouts.

Painting

1. Base-coat areas: *stocking cuffs:* white; *puppy stocking:* tompte red; *puppy stocking heel and toe:* eucalyptus; *puppy:* Dresden flesh; *puppy's spots:* brown; *puppy's bow:* eucalyptus; *kitty stocking:* eucalyptus; *kitty stocking heel and toe:* tompte red; *kitty face:* white; *kitty:* Dresden flesh, then base-coat again using a mixture of 60 percent glaze base and 40 percent clay; *kitty's nose:* pink; *kitty's bow:* tompte red.

2. *Shade designs, working on small areas at a time:* Load filbert brush with a small amount of paint, then stroke on palette to remove some of color. Referring to patterns, apply paints to areas to be shaded. Quickly stroke brush on paper towel, then pat dry brush on applied paint to soften and blend; patting is the key to success. Allow

to dry, then repeat as needed to darken. Shade as follows: *stocking cuffs:* gray; let dry, then shade again lightly with brown; *puppy stocking:* barn red; let dry, then shade again lightly with brown; *puppy stocking heel and toe:* hunter green; *puppy:* brown; *puppy's bow:* hunter green; *kitty stocking:* hunter green; let dry and then shade again lightly with brown; *kitty stocking heel and toe:* barn red; *kitty:* brown; *kitty's bow:* barn red.

3. *Blush cheeks:* Load filbert brush with a small amount of mauve paint; stroke on paper towel until dry, and then pat dry brush on cheeks. There will be enough paint residue left in bristles to add soft color.

4. *Lining:* Pull #1 liner through pool of paint, twirling as you go until bristles form a point. Use flowing strokes, making sure bristles are vertical, not on their sides. Use just the tip of the bristles, as you would a pencil. Line as follows: *puppy stocking cuff:* hunter green; *kitty stocking cuff:* barn red; *kitty's stripes:* stroke in lines using #3 round brush with clay.

Finishing

1. Using fine tip of marker, outline designs. Do not outline puppy's spots or kitty's stripes. Fill in puppy's nose darkly.

2. Apply two coats varnish to front, back and sides of each ornament.

3. Add ribbon hanging loop to each ornament. ❋

Sleepy Puppy

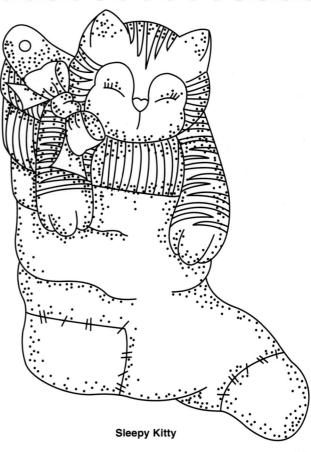

Sleepy Kitty

Gingerbread Kids

You can almost taste warm gingerbread as you assemble this boy-and-girl couple! Hang them from the tree to sweeten your day.

Designs by Helen Rafson

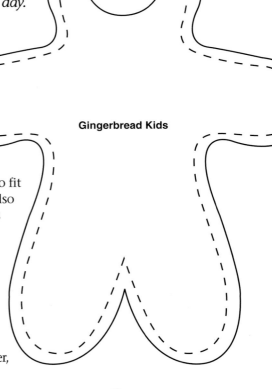

Gingerbread Kids

Materials

Both Ornaments

- Fusible webbing
- Tan print fabric
- Heavy brown paper or paper bag
- 12" white baby rickrack
- Scraps of construction paper: brown, pink, red
- Hole punch
- 7/16" flat four-hole buttons: 2 brown, 2 pink
- 6" 1/4"-wide pink satin ribbon
- Natural jute twine
- Black fine-tip permanent marker*
- Titanium white acrylic paint*
- Toothpick
- Polyester fiberfill
- Craft glue
- Seam sealant
- Iron

ZIG Memory System Millennium marker from EK Success Ltd.; and Americana acrylic paint from DecoArt.

Project Notes

Refer to photo and pattern throughout.

Follow manufacturer's instructions for working with fusible webbing.

Let paint and glue dry before proceeding with next step.

Instructions

1. Tracing along dashed lines, trace two inner gingerbread shapes onto back of fusible webbing. Fuse webbing to wrong side of tan fabric; cut shapes from fused fabric.

2. Cutting on solid lines, cut four outer gingerbread shapes from heavy brown paper.

3. Peel backing from fabric shapes and fuse each in the center of a paper shape for ornament fronts.

4. *"Icing" trim:* Cut rickrack to fit across fabric arms and legs; also cut a piece to fit around girl's neckline. Treat ends of rickrack with seam sealant; let dry. Glue rickrack in place.

5. Using marker, draw smile on each ornament front.

6. *Cheeks and eyes:* Using hole punch, punch four circles from brown construction paper, two circles from red and two

"S'more" Snowman

Hang this tasty treat on the tree to remind your family of warm memories of summer!

Design by Missy Becker

Want s'more?

Materials

- 2 (2½") squares corrugated cardboard
- Craft foam: brown and white
- Air-dry modeling compound*
- 4 (1½") pieces 24-gauge black wire
- 8" jute
- Tacky craft glue
- Toothpick
- Acrylic paints*: pumpkin, lamp black, light cinnamon
- Paintbrushes: #10 shader, #4 round, #0 liner

Delight modeling compound from Creative Paperclay; and Americana acrylic paints from DecoArt.

Project Notes

Refer to photo throughout.

Refer to manufacturer's instructions for working with air-dry modeling compound.

Instructions

1. *Graham crackers:* Corrugated cardboard squares will be top and bottom "graham crackers." On top cracker, float line of cinnamon down the center. Dip handle of paintbrush into cinnamon and place six dots on each side of line, like perforations on a graham cracker.

2. *Chocolate:* Cut 1½" x 2" rectangle brown craft foam. Glue onto bottom cracker leaving a cardboard margin of only ¼" showing at front of cracker.

3. *Melted marshmallow:* Cut a "puddle" of white craft foam that will fit on top of brown foam without covering it; this will be melted bottom of marshmallow snowman.

4. *Marshmallow snowman:* Pinch off clay about the size of a marble for body; roll into ball. Pinch off

another piece smaller than the first for head; roll into a ball and lightly press onto body. Let dry.

5. *Arms:* Twist together two pieces of wire, leaving about ¼" untwisted at one end and spread apart for "hands." Repeat with remaining pieces of wire. Trim arms evenly and push twisted ends into snowman.

6. *Painting:* Using toothpick dipped in black, dot on eyes, mouth and buttons. Using round brush, paint nose with pumpkin.

7. *Assembly:* Glue snowman in center of white puddle. Glue back edge of top cracker to back edge of bottom cracker and to top of snowman's head. (Floated center line should be on top of cracker, and should run from front to back, not side to side.)

8. *Hanger:* Apply a little glue to ends of jute. Using toothpick, push ends into corrugated grooves in center of front edge of top cracker; let glue dry before hanging ornament.

Optional: If desired, add a little paper tag printed with "Want S'more?" to ornament. ❂

Gingerbread Kids

from pink. Glue pink circles at ends of girl's smile for cheeks; glue on two brown circles for eyes. Using marker, add eyelashes to girl. Glue red circles at ends of boy's smile; glue on remaining brown circles for eyes.

7. Using toothpick dipped in white

paint, add tiny highlight dot near edge of each cheek and eye.

8. *"Stuffing":* Glue a small amount of fiberfill to back of each ornament front, avoiding edges; let dry. Run a thin bead of glue around edges on wrong side of gingerbread girl; glue to one of the plain brown paper shapes. Repeat with boy and remaining paper shape.

9. Tie ribbon in a bow; trim ends and treat with seam sealant; let dry. Glue at girl's neckline; glue pink buttons down girl's front. Tie a bow from twine; frizz ends and glue at boy's neckline. Glue brown buttons down his front.

10. *Hanging loops:* Cut two 9" pieces twine; fold in half and glue cut ends to backs of ornaments. ❂

Begging for Christmas

This patient little doggie is just begging to be hung on your tree this Christmas!

Design by Jackie Haskell

Materials

- Polymer clay*: white, red, black, tan, ivory brilliant
- 2 (3mm) black round ball beads
- 1½" 24-gauge wire
- Straight-edge tool
- Straight pin
- Clean white rag or fabric napkin
- Oven-proof plate
- Oven

Sculpey III polymer clay.

Project Notes

Refer to photo throughout.

Clean all traces of color from fingers with white rag or napkin before working with next color.

Use a pin to remove any pieces of lint or fibers that stick to the clay, then smooth clay with fingers to remove pin marks.

Instructions

1. *Body:* Cut a quarter-section from brick of ivory compound, then cut that piece in half. Reserve one half for face; soften other half and roll it into a ball, then form into 1¾" teardrop, keeping the back flat by shaping it on a flat surface. With thumb and forefinger, pinch indentations into rounded end of teardrop where legs will be attached later.

2. *Arms:* Cut a marble-size ball of ivory in half; roll each into a ball, then shape each into a 1" log; flatten ends slightly and attach one end of each to pointed part of body.

3. *Hind legs:* Roll marble-size ball of ivory; cut in half and use one half for each leg. Form each into an

oblong circle and attach to body at indentations formed in step 1.

4. *Feet:* Cut a pea-size ball of ivory compound in half; form each into a slightly flattened teardrop shape. Attach each foot by placing pointed end under hind leg. Using straight-edge tool, make two indentations for toes in front edge of each foot.

5. *Head:* Cut reserved section of ivory compound (step 1) in half; use one half for head, rolling it first into a ball and then into an egg shape. Smaller end will be top of head. From a small amount of tan, make a "spot" and place on head where one eye will be. Push beads into face for eyes, pushing them in on their sides until none of bead hole is visible. Using straight pin, indent two eyelashes at outer corner of eyes; add light vertical line down center of fat end of head. Rub red compound with little finger; apply a little bit of color to cheeks. Roll a very tiny ball of black; attach to tip of nose. Attach head to body firmly but carefully. Position arms in begging position and, with straight-edge tool, make two indentations for toes in front edge of each paw.

6. *Ears:* Form a pea-size ball each of tan and ivory; shape and flatten into teardrops. Attach pointed ends of ears to sides of head and let ears hang down.

7. *Tail:* Form a half-pea-size ball of ivory into a 1" cone and attach broad end to back of body. Attach remainder of tail along one side of body.

8. *Spots:* Make spots from tan compound in different sizes, flattening them and varying their shapes. Press spots onto body.

9. *Hat:* For trim, form a half-marble-size ball of white into a 1½" rope; for pompom, roll half-pea-size ball of white into a ball. Set white pieces aside. Cut quarter-section from red compound brick; cut off one-eighth from this piece and use it for hat. Roll it into a ball, then shape it into a cone. Slightly flatten the fatter end; place on head and fold point of hat over to one side. Clean hands thoroughly to remove all traces of red color before proceeding. Wrap white trim around base of hat; attach pompom to tip.

10. *Hanger:* Bend wire into a U-shape and press ends into top of hat.

11. *Baking:* Place dog on oven-proof plate; bake in preheated 275-degree oven for 10 minutes. Let cool completely. ❈

Santa's Little Helper

Here's a sweet little elf to bring color and fun to your miniature Christmas tree.

Design by Jackie Haskell

Materials
- Polymer clay*: yellow, red, beige, lime
- 2 black seed beads
- 1¼" 24-gauge wire
- Straight-edge tool
- Straight pin
- Clean white rag or fabric napkin
- Oven-proof plate
- Oven

Sculpey III polymer clay.

Project Notes

Refer to photo throughout.

Clean all traces of color from fingers with white rag or napkin before working with next color.

Use a pin to remove any pieces of lint or fibers that stick to the clay, then smooth clay with fingers to remove pin marks.

Instructions

1. *Body/hat:* Cut a quarter-section from brick of lime compound, then cut that piece in half. Soften one half and roll it into a ball, then form into 1¾" teardrop, keeping the back flat by shaping it on a flat surface. Wipe any green color from fingers before proceeding.

2. *Face:* Make a pea-size ball of beige; cut in half. Use half for the face and save other half for the hands. Flatten face portion into a circle and position halfway down side of body. Push beads into the face for eyes, pushing them in on their sides until none of bead hole is visible. Rub red compound with little finger; apply a little bit of color to cheeks. Attach a tiny ball of beige to face for nose. Using pin, indent two eyelashes at outer corner of eyes, and add smile.

3. *Hair:* Shape pea-size ball of yellow into a 2" rope. From this piece, cut six equal pieces for sides and three shorter equal pieces for bangs. (You may need to reshape these after they have been cut.) Attach bangs, then attach three of the larger pieces to each side of head.

4. *Arms, hands, wrist trim:* Cut a pea-size ball of lime in half; use one half for each arm. Shape each into a ¼" log. Cut the reserved half-pea of beige (step 2) in half; roll each into a ball and place at ends of arms for hands; slightly flatten other ends of arms. For wrist trim, form a pea-size ball of red; cut in quarters. Take one of those quarters and cut it in half; form each tiny piece into a rope long enough to go around half of each wrist. Attach trim where arms and hands meet. Attach arms to body.

5. *Buttons:* Form two very small balls of red; attach to body between hands. Add buttonholes to each with point of pin.

6. *Shoes:* Form each shoe from a pea-size ball of red; shape each into a slightly flattened ½"-long teardrop. Attach rounded ends to body with shoes pointing out. Using straight edge, indent line for heels in bottoms of shoes. Attach a tiny ball of lime to tip of each shoe.

7. *Hat trim:* Form a pea-size ball of red into a 1½" rope; attach to body/hat so that trim covers top of hair. Bend tip of hat forward; attach a ball formed from one-quarter of a pea-size ball of red to tip of hat. Remove any red color from hands before proceeding.

8. *Hanger:* Bend wire into a U-shape and press ends into top of elf.

9. *Baking:* Place elf on oven-proof plate; bake in preheated 275-degree oven for 10 minutes. Let cool completely. ❈

Christmas Mouse

This tiny mouse is holding a candy cane just for you. Hang him on a branch for that special little touch!

Design by Jackie Haskell

Materials

- Polymer clay*: white, red, dusty rose, lime
- 2 (3mm) black round ball beads
- 1¼" 24-gauge wire
- Straight-edge tool
- Straight pin
- Clean white rag or fabric napkin
- Oven-proof plate
- Oven

Sculpey III polymer clay.

Project Notes

Refer to photo throughout.

Clean all traces of color from fingers with white rag or napkin before working with next color.

Use a pin to remove any pieces of lint or fibers that stick to the clay, then smooth clay with fingers to remove pin marks.

Instructions

1. *Body:* Cut a quarter-section from brick of white compound, then cut that piece in half. Soften one half and roll it into a teardrop. With thumb and forefinger, pinch indentations into fat end of teardrop where legs will be attached later.

2. *Arms:* Form two pea-size balls of white, one for each arm. Form each into a ½" log; flatten slightly and attach one end of each to pointed part of body.

3. *Legs:* Roll marble-size ball of white; cut in half and use one half for each leg. Form each into a ¾" log, then turn up ¼" at end of each to form foot. Continue forming feet. Slightly flatten other end of legs and press into body at indentations formed in step 1.

4. *Head:* Shape a marble-size ball of white into a teardrop; do not flatten it. Turn up pointed end of teardrop to form nose. Push beads on edge into the face for eyes until none of bead hole is visible. Rub red compound with your little finger; apply a little bit of color to cheeks. Using pin, indent two eyelashes at outer corner of eyes, and eyebrows; add vertical line down from tip of nose. Roll a very tiny ball of rose; attach to tip of nose.

5. *Ears:* Cut a pea-size ball of white in half. Slightly flatten each into a circle; attach to head.

6. *Tail:* Form a pea-size ball of white into a 1½" rope. Attach one end to back of body and curve the rest of the tail up onto body. Remove white coloring from fingers before proceeding. Roll four tiny balls of rose; flatten two for ear centers and attach to ears; flatten other two into teardrop shapes for bottoms of feet and press into place, points down. Using straight-edge tool, indent fingers/toes in edges of paws and feet.

7. *Candy cane:* Cut a half-marble-size ball each of white and red; form each into 1½" rope. Make a 1½" rope from a pea-size ball of lime. Twist all three ropes together; curve over one end to make candy cane and place in mouse's arms.

8. *Wreath:* Form half of a pea-size ball of lime into a 2¾" rope; fold in half with ends even and twist. Form into a circle and place on mouse's head over right ear, concealing ends behind ear. Roll six very tiny balls of red; attach to wreath in clusters of three.

9. *Baking:* Place mouse on oven-proof plate; bake in preheated 275-degree oven for 10 minutes. Let cool completely. ✽

Fan Ornaments

These old-fashioned fans accented in gold will add a lovely touch to any tree.

Design by Mary Ayres

Materials
Both Ornaments
- 2 (4") paper fans*
- 2 (20") pieces 20-gauge gold wire
- 1 yard ⅜"-wide wire-edge gold metallic ribbon
- Shape motifs stencil*
- Acrylic paints*: lavender, desert turquoise, true red, glorious gold metallic
- Paintbrushes: #5 natural hair bristle, ¼" stencil brush
- Extra-fine-tip opaque gold writer*
- Glue*
- Craft drill and ³⁄₃₂" bit
- Scrap wood

Paper fans from Nicole Industries; Simply Stencils motif stencil #28209 from Plaid; Americana and Dazzling Metallics acrylic paints from DecoArt; ZIG Memory System writer from EK Success Ltd.; and Kids Choice Glue from Beacon.

Project Notes

Refer to photo throughout.

See directions for stenciling and dry-brushing under "Painting Techniques" in the General Instructions, page 190.

Let all paints and glue dry between applications.

Instructions

1. Drill a hole about ¼" from end of each wooden spine at ends of fan (when fan is closed, the top and bottom spines). *Note: Lay spine flat on a piece of scrap wood before drilling to keep drill bit from splitting or breaking fan.* Repeat with second fan.

2. Using turquoise and stencil brush, stencil curl shapes, evenly spaced and pointing in all directions, on one side of one fan. In same manner, stencil flower shapes on one side of second fan, using red for petal shapes and lavender for flower centers.

3. Dry-brush top edges of both fans with gold.

4. Using paintbrush handle dipped in gold, place a dot of paint in center of each curl, in center of each flower, and between stenciled motifs on both fans.

5. Using gold writer, draw "running stitch" around edge of each motif and again around each motif ⅛" from first line of "stitches." In same manner, add single line of "running stitches" along bottom and side edges of each fan.

6. Cut ribbon in half; tie each in a simple bow. Turn fans upside down and glue bows to center of wooden strips, arranging streamers as desired.

7. *Hangers:* Curl each piece of wire around a pencil; slide off and expand curls. Insert ends of one wire through holes in fan and twist wire ends to secure. Adjust curled wire in an arc over fan. Repeat with remaining wire and fan. ❁

Holiday Stockings

Give your tree a beautiful look with this lovely pair of painted stockings.
The holly and flowers add a pretty touch to these Christmas socks.

Designs by Vicki Schreiner

Materials
Both Ornaments

- Felt*: 9" x 12" sheet antique white; 3" square each plush cranberry and plush hunter green
- Coordinating 6-strand cotton embroidery floss: dark green and dark red
- Coordinating ¼"-wide decorative braid: 7" each dark green and dark red
- Embroidery and large-eye needles
- 2 (8") pieces gold metallic cord
- Polyester fiberfill
- Fabric adhesive*
- Textile medium*
- Acrylic paints*: tompte red, empire gold, hunter green, barn red, eucalyptus
- Paintbrushes: #3 round, #1 liner, #4 shader
- 1 sheet plain paper

Rainbow Classic and Plush felts from Kunin; Fabri-Tac Adhesive from Beacon; and Ceramcoat textile medium and acrylic paints from Delta.

Project Notes

Refer to photo, patterns and painting diagrams throughout.

Use 6 strands floss for all blanket stitch.

Mix equal amounts paint with textile medium for all painting.

Refer to instructions for base-coating under "Painting Techniques" in the General Instructions, page 190.

Allow all paints to dry between steps.

Stockings

1. Cut two stockings from antique white felt for each ornament. Using green floss for Stocking 1 and red floss for Stocking 2, blanket-stitch stockings together in pairs, stitching down one side, across bottom and back up other side, leaving top edges open.

2. Cut one heel pattern and one toe pattern from plain paper. Lay cutouts on felt stocking ornament; using pencil, trace inside curved line of heel and toe onto felt; these lines will serve as painting guides. Repeat on other ornament.

3. *Cuffs:* Fold cranberry felt square in half wrong sides facing to form pocket that will fit over top of ornament. Apply a small bead of adhesive down inside of left outer edge of cuff from fold down; press and hold together until dry. Repeat down inside right edge. Repeat with green felt square.

4. *Hanging loops:* Thread one strand

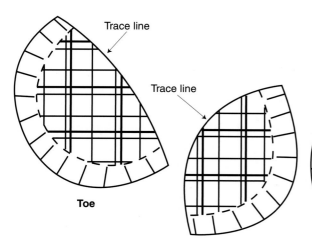

Trace line

Trace line

Toe

Heel

Stocking
Cut 2 from antique white felt tor each ornament

of gold cord onto large-eye needle. Working at top right corner of cuff, insert needle through cuff from inside to outside. Wiggle needle to enlarge insertion hole and pull cord through hole, leaving a cord tail inside cuff. Insert needle again from outside to inside through a second hole about ⅛" from first; pull needle and cord through, leaving a 2½" hanging loop outside cuff. Knot cord ends together inside cuff; trim off excess cord. Using scissors, slightly round the top corners of cuff. Repeat to add hanging loop to second cuff.

5. *Stuffing:* Stuff each stocking lightly with fiberfill. Apply a narrow bead of adhesive inside top edges; press edges together to glue tops of stockings shut; hold until glue dries.

6. *Cuffs and trim:* Place cranberry cuff over top of Stocking 1 (with green blanket stitch) and green cuff over top of Stocking 2 (red blanket stitch). Apply a small bead of adhesive inside cuffs on front and back; press cuffs to stockings and hold in place until dry. Matching color of trim to cuff, glue braid trim around bottom edge of each cuff, trimming ends neatly and positioning ends at center back.

Painting

1. Base-coat heel and toe areas of Stocking 1 (cranberry cuff) with tompte red; base-coat heel and toe of Stocking 2 (green cuff) with hunter green.

2. Following step-by-step Stocking Painting Diagrams, paint designs as directed below for individual designs.

Stocking 1

1. Using liner brush, line first stem with hunter green.

2. Add small leaves with hunter green, working strokes from outside and pulling toward stem.

3. Line second stem with hunter green; add small leaves with eucalyptus.

4. Line third stem with hunter green; add small leaves with eucalyptus. Shade all leaves by dabbing a small amount of hunter green on each leaf near stem.

5. Dot three large tompte red berries onto center area of leaves.

Stocking 2

1. Using #3 round brush, paint three small leaves with eucalyptus; shade leaves by dabbing a small amount of hunter green on each leaf.

2. Using barn red, paint three background flowers, working strokes from outside and pulling toward center of flowers.

3. Using tompte red, paint two foreground flowers and one partial flower peeking out from right leaf.

4. Using gold, paint three small dots in center of each flower; using liner, add hunter green veins to leaves. ❋

Painting diagrams on page 105

Felt Birds

Sew a flock of these colorful winged friends to hang from the branches.
Tie one on a package for that extra crafty touch.

Design by Chris Malone

Materials
Each Ornament

- Felt*: 1 sheet lime, red, lavender or neon blue; plus scrap antique gold
- Metallic embroidery floss*: green #5269, red #5270, purple #5289 or electric blue #5290; plus gold #5284
- Gold sewing thread
- Embroidery needle
- 2 (3mm) gold glass beads
- 18" ⅜"-wide metallic gold wire-edge ribbon
- 4½"–5" forked twig
- Gold spray paint*
- 8" fine gold cord
- Polyester fiberfill
- Thick craft glue or hot-glue gun

Rainbow Classic Felt from Kunin; DMC metallic embroidery floss and Crafter's gold spray paint from Krylon.

Project Notes

Refer to patterns and photo throughout.

Use 2 strands floss for all stitching.

Felt Bird

1. Cut two birds and two wings from either lime, red, lavender or blue felt; cut two beaks from gold.

2. Using gold floss, blanket-stitch beaks together along curved sides, leaving straight side open; stuff beak lightly with fiberfill.

3. Pin birds together, inserting open edge of beak where indicated by dots on pattern. Using matching floss, blanket-stitch all around bird, stuffing lightly before closing completely and catching beak in stitches.

4. Using matching floss, blanket-stitch wings together, stuffing lightly before closing completely.

5. Using sewing thread, sew one

bead "eye" to front of head where indicated by X on pattern, pulling thread to indent eye slightly; add second eye on back of bird. Knot thread; clip ends.

6. Glue wing to front of bird.

Finishing Ornament

1. Spray all surfaces of twig with paint; let dry. Glue branch along back of bird near bottom.

2. Tie ribbon around twig in a bow just behind bird. Tie a knot 1" from

end of each streamer; notch ends of streamers. Loop streamers around twig on both sides of bow, using dots of glue to hold loops in place.

3. *Hanging loop*: Run gold cord

through top edge of bird near wing; knot ends to make hanging loop. Pull loop so knot is concealed on back of bird; secure with a dot of glue. ❁

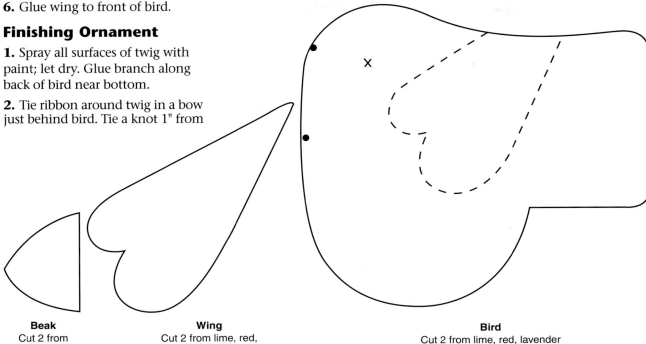

Beak
Cut 2 from
antique gold felt

Wing
Cut 2 from lime, red,
lavender or neon blue felt

Bird
Cut 2 from lime, red, lavender
or neon blue felt

Holiday Stockings

Continued from page 103

Stocking Painting Diagram—Stocking 1 (Red Cuff)

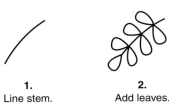

1.
Line stem.

2.
Add leaves.

3.
Add second
stem of leaves.

4.
Add third
stem of leaves.

5.
Add berries.

Stocking Painting Diagram—Stocking 2 (Green Cuff)

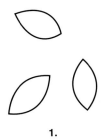

1.
Apply 3 leaves.

2.
Add 3 background
flowers.

3.
Add 2 foreground
flowers, and 1 half-flower
to right leaf.

4.
Add 3 dots to
center of each
flower. Line leaves.

Paper Ornaments

Put a little bit of your heart into each of these paper Christmas shapes.

Designs by Mary Ayres

Materials
- Sparkle paper: purple, yellow, green, light pink, orange
- Gold translucent vellum*
- Card stock: red, white
- Black fine-tip writer*
- 2-way glue*
- Paper-crafting products*: pinking paper edgers, heart-shape paper punch, 1/16" circle hand punch
- 5 (10") pieces metallic gold pearl cotton

Translucent vellum from Chartham Shimmering Metallics; ZIG Memory System writer and 2-Way Glue from EK Success Ltd.; and Fiskars paper-crafting products.

Project Note
Refer to photo and patterns throughout.

Instructions

1. Using scissors, cut shapes along dashed lines from sparkle papers, cutting house from purple, star from yellow, tree from green, heart from light pink and gingerbread boy from orange.

2. For each shape, cut a center heart from red card stock. Using black writer, draw simulated "blanket stitches" around edges of hearts; glue a heart to center of each sparkling shape.

3. Using heart punch, punch five hearts from vellum. Glue one in center of each red heart. Using black writer, draw simulated "running stitch" around each vellum heart on red heart.

4. Using pinking paper edgers and cutting along solid lines, cut one of each shape from white card stock. Using black writer through step 5, draw simulated "blanket stitches" around edges of white shapes with stitches pointing out between pinked points.

5. Glue sparkling shapes in centers of matching white shapes. Draw simulated "running stitch" on white card stock close to edges of each sparkling shape.

6. *Hanging loops:* Using 1/16" round punch, punch hole in center top of each ornament. Thread a piece of pearl cotton through each hole and knot ends. ❉

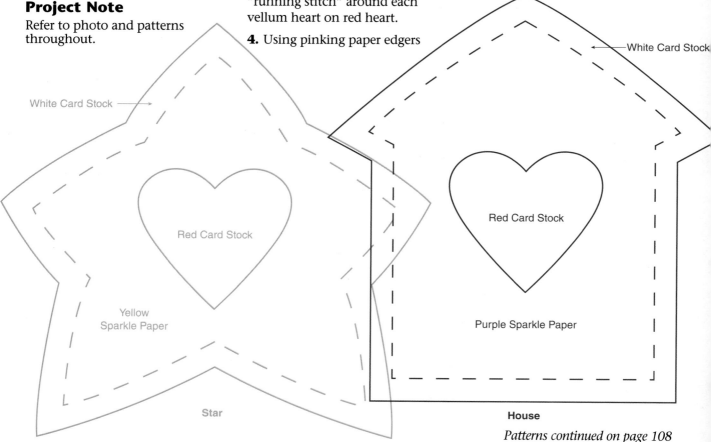

White Card Stock

Red Card Stock

Yellow Sparkle Paper

Star

White Card Stock

Red Card Stock

Purple Sparkle Paper

House

Patterns continued on page 108

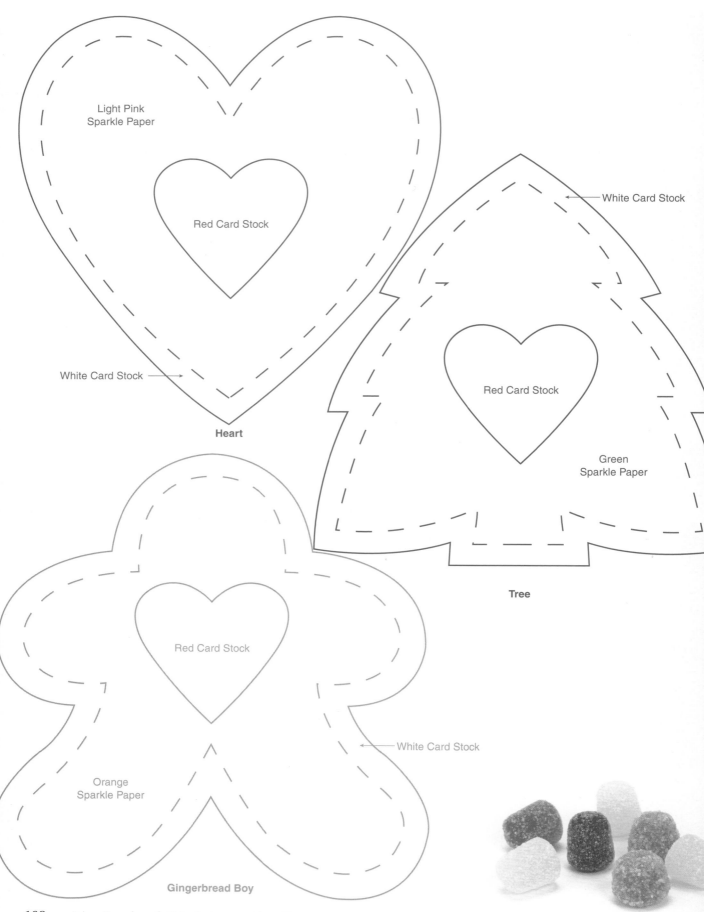

Light Pink
Sparkle Paper

Red Card Stock

White Card Stock

Heart

White Card Stock

Red Card Stock

Green
Sparkle Paper

Tree

Red Card Stock

White Card Stock

Orange
Sparkle Paper

Gingerbread Boy

Craft Stick Rudolph

Making this sad-looking reindeer will surely warm your heart and bring a smile to your face.

Design by Missy Becker

Materials

- Mini craft stick
- ¼" wooden furniture plug
- 1" wooden heart cutout
- 1¼" x ⅜" wooden wings
- Mini (1⅛" x 1⅝") twig bow
- Acrylic paints*: titanium white, sable brown, burnt umber, lamp black, Napa red
- Paintbrushes: #10 shader, #5 round, #0 liner
- 6" natural raffia
- 1" imitation tiny holly garland
- 3 red metallic beads
- Cotton-tip swab
- 1" pin back
- Tacky craft glue

Americana acrylic paints from DecoArt.

Project Notes

Refer to photo and patterns throughout.

Paint all surfaces of wooden pieces.

Let paints dry between applications.

Instructions

Body/Legs

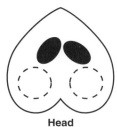

Head

1. Paint wooden furniture plug (nose) red; paint all other wooden pieces brown.

2. Dip cotton-tipped swab in red; remove excess paint on paper towel and "scrub" cheeks onto head (wooden heart) in area indicated by dashed lines on pattern.

3. Using round brush dipped in black, paint eyes and hooves.

4. Pick up small amount of burnt umber on corner of shader brush; float line up center of craft stick to define legs.

5. Using toothpick dipped in white, add highlight dot to each eye. Thin a little white with water until it is of an inky consistency; using liner brush, add comma-stroke highlight across top of nose with thinned mixture.

6. Glue wings (ears) to back of heart near top; glue nose to face. Turn twig bow upside down; glue at top of heart for antlers.

7. Glue tiny garland to front of antlers; add beads for "holly berries." Tie small bow from raffia; glue to body just below head.

8. Glue pin back vertically to back of body. ❊

Candle Cup Ornaments

The kids will love hanging these festive trims on your tree!

Frosty will warm your heart while the soldier boy keeps the order on your tree!

Designs by Dorothy Egan

Materials

Each Ornament

- 1½" x 1½" wooden candle cup
- 1¼" wooden ball knob
- Paintbrushes: #4 and #8 flats, fine liner
- 7" ⅛"-wide red satin ribbon
- Hot-glue gun
- White craft glue

Soldier

- 4" ⅛"-wide black velvet ribbon
- Acrylic paints*: titanium white, lamp black, medium flesh, blush flesh, brilliant red, glorious gold metallic

Snowman

- ⅜" x 2½" strip plaid fabric or knit fabric cut from old sweater
- 2 (½") red pompoms
- Acrylic paints*: titanium white, moon yellow, burnt orange, country red, mistletoe, lamp black
- Wooden round toothpick
- Fine-point black permanent marking pen

Americana and Dazzling Metallics acrylic paints from DecoArt.

Project Notes

Refer to pattern and photo throughout.

Paint all surfaces of wooden pieces.

Refer to directions for base-coating and rouging under "Painting Techniques" in the General Instructions, page 190.

Let all paints and glue dry between applications.

Soldier

1. Base-coat candle cup with red and ball knob with medium flesh.

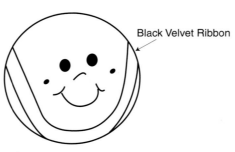

Black Velvet Ribbon

Candle Cup Soldier

2. *Head:* Rouge cheeks with blush flesh. Using liner, paint nose and mouth with a mixture of blush flesh and red. Using tip of paintbrush handle dipped in black, dot on eyes; add tiny highlight dot of white to each eye and cheek.

3. *Hat:* Paint ⅛" stripe of black around body of candle cup right next to rim. Paint plume area with a combination of black and white; stroke over plume area with undiluted white to define "feathers." Paint brim area and plume holder with gold. Using liner, lightly outline feather edges and gold plume holder.

4. *Hanger:* Knot ends of ribbon together; insert loop through hole in candle cup from inside to outside. Pull knot snug against inside of candle cup and hot-glue to secure.

5. *Chin strap:* Cut a strip of black

Continued on page 115

Tin-Punch Elfin Ornament

This painted tin-punch elf is a perfect gift for a favorite teacher, day-care provider or another cherished "helper."

Design by Sandra Graham Smith

Materials

- 5" x 6" piece aluminum flashing
- Tin snips
- Pressed-wood board
- Fine-point permanent markers: black, red
- Enamel paints: red, white, green, pink
- Assorted small paintbrushes
- Tracing paper
- Masking tape
- Finishing nails
- Large nail
- Hammer
- 12" black embroidery floss
- 8mm silver bell

Project Notes

Aluminum flashing is widely available at hardware stores.

Refer to photo and pattern throughout.

Tin-Punch Elfin Ornament

Instructions

1. Trace pattern onto tracing paper; trace outline onto aluminum. Cut out with tin snips.

2. Tape paper pattern to aluminum. Place on pressed-wood board. Punch design using finishing nails and hammer, moving from dot to dot. Space holes evenly and replace finishing nail when point dulls.

3. Using larger nail and hammer, punch larger hole in top of elf's hat for attaching hanger and in tip of hat for attaching bell.

4. Remove pattern and tape. Turn aluminum shape over; smooth side is back of project.

5. Apply paint inside punched lines using thick strokes: *Hat and collar:* green; *hat brim:* white; *face:* pink; *cheeks:* dark pink (blend a little red into pink for a darker shade); *hair:* red. Let dry.

6. Draw eyes, nose and freckles with black marker. Using red marker, draw mouth.

7. Thread black embroidery floss through larger hole at top of hat for hanger. Tie bell through hole in tip of hat with embroidery floss. ❈

Winter Hats

Frame photos of loved ones of all ages with these colorful hats.
They're a great way to personalize your family's tree!

Designs by Missy Becker

Materials
All Frames
- ⅛" basswood stock
- Acrylic paints*: titanium white, cadmium yellow, boysenberry pink, lavender, Williamsburg blue, lamp black, sapphire, ultra blue deep, soft black, Napa red, khaki tan, asphaltum
- Paintbrushes: #10 shader, #5 round, #0 liner
- 3 (6") pieces ⅛"-wide white satin ribbon
- Hot-glue gun
- Graphite paper
- Sandpaper
- Craft saw

Americana acrylic paints from DecoArt.

Project Notes
Refer to photo and patterns throughout.

To transfer patterns, refer to instructions for "Using Transfer & Graphite Paper" in the General Instructions, page 190.

Paint all surfaces of hat ornaments; back and edges can be painted in a single base color and details added only to front, if desired.

See directions for floating under "Painting Techniques" in the General Instructions, page 190.

Let all paints dry between applications.

Preparation
1. Transfer desired hat pattern to basswood stock using graphite paper.

Using craft saw, carefully cut out center opening, then cut outline of hat.

2. Sand edges of wood ornament.

3. Paint individual designs according to following instructions.

Blue Knit Hat
1. Paint all surfaces of hat with sapphire.

2. Thin a little ultra blue deep to an inky consistency with water. Using liner brush, add detail lines to hat and scarf with mixture.

3. Thin a little white to an inky consistency with water. Using liner and thinned mixture, add detail lines next to lines added in step 2. Also line fuzzy pompom on top of hat.

4. Dip corner of shader in ultra

blue deep; float shading along edges of scarf, at base of hat brim, and at base of hat crown.

Striped Stocking Hat

1. Paint ribbon ties on sides of hat, bow and every fourth stripe on hat with pink.

2. Paint hat brim and stripes to left of pink stripes with lavender. Paint stripes to left of lavender stripes with ultra blue deep; paint remaining stripes with yellow.

3. Paint pompom white. Thin a little white to an inky consistency with water; using

liner, line lavender ribbing on hat brim with mixture. Dip corner of shader into diluted mixture; float highlights on top of bow loops and bow center knot.

4. Dip corner of shader brush in soft black; float shading on bottom of lavender hat brim, and along bottom edge of "tail" of hat.

5. Dip corner of shader brush in

Williamsburg blue; float shading along bottom of white pompom.

6. Dip corner of shader brush in red; float shading on bow and ribbon ties.

Tan Earflap Hat

1. Paint all surfaces of hat with tan. Paint hat brim and scarf with red.

2. Thin a little white to an inky consistency with water; using round brush and liner brush, add pattern of plaid lines on scarf with mixture.

3. Dip corner of shader brush in white; float highlights on hat and scarf.

4. Dip corner of shader brush in asphaltum; float shading along edges of hat.

5. Dip corner of shader brush in lamp black; float shading along edges of scarf.

Finishing

1. *Hanging loop:* Fold a piece of ribbon in half; glue ends to back of ornament at center top.

2. Glue photo in opening in hat frame. ❀

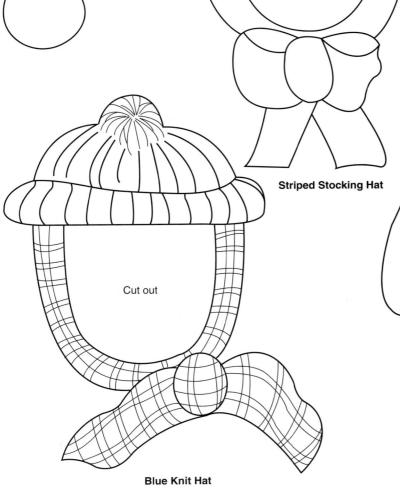

Striped Stocking Hat

Blue Knit Hat

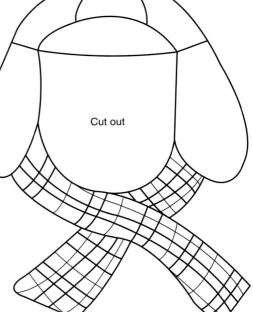

Tan Earflap Hat

Holiday Birdhouse

This little bird will be pleased to make your tree his home for the winter.
His birdhouse is even decorated for the holidays!

Design by Maggie Rampy

Materials

- Wooden 1¾" x 2" A-frame birdhouse*
- Decorative snow*
- 1" mini mushroom bird
- Acrylic paints*: Wedgewood blue, sable brown, evergreen, silver sage green, soft black, light buttermilk, golden straw, Santa red, green mist
- Paintbrushes: ¼" angular, #2 script liner, #00 fabric spotter
- Graphite paper
- Stylus
- Medium-grit sandpaper
- Tack cloth
- ½" transparent tape
- ³⁄₁₆" eye screw
- 6" ⅛"-wide red satin ribbon
- White craft glue

Birdhouse from Weston Bowl Mill; Americana Snow-Tex decorative snow and acrylic paints from DecoArt.

Project Notes

Refer to photo and patterns throughout.

To transfer patterns, refer to instructions for "Using Transfer & Graphite Paper" in the General Instructions, page 190.

Let all paints, glue and decorative snow dry between applications.

Refer to manufacturer's instructions for working with decorative snow and for drying time.

Preparation & Initial Painting

1. Sand entire birdhouse; wipe off with tack cloth. Paint entire birdhouse with a coat of silver green. Sand lightly and wipe with tack cloth.

2. Apply two coats silver green to front, back and bottom of birdhouse.

3. Mask off sides of birdhouse under roof overhang with transparent tape; paint roof, including underside of overhang, with two coats brown.

4. Screw eye screw into top ridge of roof in center.

Detail Painting

1. Using stylus and graphite paper, transfer door pattern to front of house. Paint door hinge lines with liner and black; using stylus dipped in black, add tiny dot at each end of each hinge. Using handle of script liner dipped in black, dot on doorknob.

2. Transfer shingle pattern to each side of roof. Using angular brush and black, apply a "shaky" float line along bottoms of each of three rows of shingles; using script liner, add individual vertical divisions to

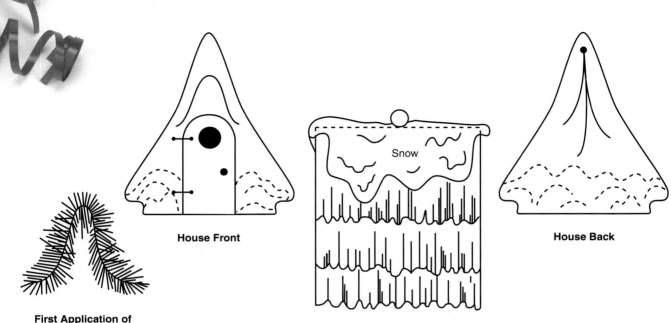

House Front

First Application of Evergreen Needles

Snow

Shingle Design

House Back

define shingles; then add lighter lines to shingles to give roof a weathered look.

3. Transfer greens patterns on front and back of house. Apply pine needles with script liner, applying most with evergreen, then half as many with green mist, and finally a few with buttermilk.

4. Add bushes on front and back with spotter, first applying

evergreen, then green mist and, finally, buttermilk.

5. Add small ornaments to garlands on front and back with small end of stylus dipped in red, straw and Wedgewood blue paints, double-dotting ornaments and letting them dry between coats. Add slightly larger ornament at top of garland on back with end of script liner brush dipped in red.

Finishing

1. Apply decorative snow to top of roof with brush or small knife; let dry.

2. Thread ribbon through screw eye; knot ends together for hanging loop.

3. Glue bird to front of roof over snow, holding bird in place for several seconds until glue holds. ❆

Candle Cup Ornaments

Continued from page 110

ribbon to go around face under chin for chin strap, checking fit with candle cup hat so that ends will be concealed under hat. Glue in place with craft glue.

6. Hot-glue candle cup hat to soldier's head.

Snowman

1. Base-coat candle cup with black and ball knob with white; paint about half of toothpick burnt orange.

2. *Head*: Rouge cheeks with red. Using liner and black, add mouth. Using tip of paintbrush handle dipped in black, dot on eyes; add tiny highlight dot of white to each.

3. *Nose:* Clip about ⅜" from painted end of toothpick and glue cut end to snowman's face.

4. *Hat:* Paint ¼" stripe of red around body of candle cup right next to rim. Using small brush and mistletoe, paint a cluster of three holly leaves onto red hatband. Highlight holly leaves with a mixture of mistletoe and yellow. Dot on a cluster of three holly berries in leaves' center using paintbrush handle dipped in red. Using pen, outline berries to define them and add veins to leaves.

5. *Hanger:* Knot ends of ribbon together; insert loop through hole in candle cup from inside to outside. Pull knot snug against inside of candle cup and hot-glue to secure.

6. Hot-glue candle cup hat to snowman's head, positioning it so cluster of holly leaves is just left of center on front.

7. *Muffler and earmuffs:* Tie fabric strip around neck and glue with craft glue; glue pompoms to sides of head.

8. Dry-brush white "snow" onto hat edges, tops of earmuffs and nose. ❆

Candle Cup Snowman

Snow Angel

Wear this sweet angel on your lapel, or hang it on the tree to represent one of your little angels!

Design by Cindy Manestar

Materials

- Wooden cutouts*: large square, 2 medium circles, small teardrop, medium star
- Wooden products*: craft spoon, 2¼" scalloped wings
- Acrylic paints*: white wash, burnt orange, lamp black, French grey blue, antique deep gold, Napa red, glorious gold metallic
- Fine-point black permanent marker
- Craft cement
- Matte finish spray*
- Paintbrushes: ½" wash, #1 liner
- Wood glue
- Stylus (optional)
- Hot-glue gun
- 1¼" pin back or fine cord for hanging loop
- 6" ¼"-wide red satin ribbon

Woodsies wooden shapes and products from Forster; Americana and Dazzling Metallics acrylic paints from DecoArt; and Matte Finish Spray from Krylon.

Project Notes

Refer to photo throughout.

Paint all surfaces of all wooden pieces.

Refer to directions for base-coating and rouging under "Painting Techniques" in the General Instructions, page 190.

Let all paints, ink and finish dry between applications.

Instructions

1. *Painting:* Base-coat wooden pieces: *white:* craft spoon (head and body; "bowl" will be head) and circles (hands); *antique gold:* star (halo); *gray blue:* square (sign); *burnt orange:* teardrop (carrot nose); *glorious gold:* scalloped wings.

2. Rouge cheeks with red.

3. Using fine point of black marker, write "SNOW ANGEL" on sign, positioning it toward bottom.

4. *Assemble angel:* Using wood glue, glue wings to back of spoon; sign to front of body; hands over top corners of sign; star halo to back of head and nose to face.

5. Using fine point of black marker, outline head and body; add short marks around edges of hands and star; outline nose with short "running stitch."

6. Using stylus or paintbrush handle dipped in black, dot paint onto ends of lines of letters; dot on two eyes and a series of five dots for smile. Add short, slanted eyebrows with fine point of marker.

7. Using stylus or paintbrush handle dipped in red, place two dots side by side on sign between hands; pull paint down and together into a point to form heart.

8. Spray all surfaces of angel with one or two coats of matte finish.

9. Tie ribbon in a 1" bow; trim ends and hot-glue at neckline.

10. Using craft cement, affix pin back or hanging loop of fine cord to back of wings. ❄

Wooden Angel

Make this angel for anyone who needs a reminder of the possibility of miracles.
Her lacy wings and glittery body are simply heavenly!

Design by Sharon Tittle

Materials

- 4" wooden angel with wire hanger
- Acrylic paints*: antique white, Santa's flesh, black cherry, rose petal pink
- Glitter glaze*
- Sealer*
- Tacky craft glue
- 2" ecru crocheted heart-shaped doily
- ½" flat ivory button
- 6" ⅛"-wide ivory satin ribbon
- 2 (½") ivory ribbon roses with green ribbon "leaves"
- 30 (4mm) bone round beads*
- Fine-point black permanent marking pen
- #5 shader paintbrush

Ceramcoat acrylic paints, Glitter Glaze and sealer from Delta; and beads from The Beadery.

Project Notes

Refer to pattern and photo throughout.

Paint all surfaces of wooden angel.

Angel Face

Let all coats of paint, ink, glue, glaze and sealer dry between applications.

Instructions

1. *Paint angel: pink:* wings; *antique white:* a ¼" scalloped collar along top of body; *black cherry:* remainder of dress/body; *Santa's flesh:* head.

2. Paint a coat of glitter glaze over black cherry body.

3. Using marking pen, draw eyes and mouth on angel's face; outline wings with "running stitch" and write "Expect A Miracle" across bottom of wings.

4. Glue ribbon roses at tips of wings.

5. *Collar:* Fold doily in half, top over bottom, with rounded edges pointing down; glue at center top of dress.

Glue button over center of doily.

6. Glue beads over surface of head for hair.

7. Brush sealer over all painted areas.

8. Tie ribbon in bow at top of wire hanger; spot-glue in place. ❁

Candy Cane Snowman

Turn your favorite childhood Christmas treat into a wonderful and fun decoration to hang on your tree!

Design by Helen Rafson

Materials

- 2 (2¾") candy canes
- Craft foam: white, red, green, black
- Foam glue*
- Glue*
- Pinking shears
- Acrylic paints*: pumpkin, Christmas green, white, black, pink parfait
- Small paintbrushes
- Medium wooden teardrop*
- Flat buttons: 2 (⁷⁄₁₆") black, 2 (⁹⁄₁₆") black, ⅜" red
- White embroidery floss
- Needle
- Black fine-tip permanent marking pen
- Ribbon: 1⅞" ⅜"-wide black-and-white gingham-check, 6" ⅛"-wide gold metallic
- Tape

CraftFoam Glue and Kids Choice Glue from Beacon; Ceramcoat acrylic paints from Delta; and Woodsies teardrop from Forster.

Project Note

Refer to patterns and photo throughout. Cut pieces with regular scissors unless instructed otherwise.

Instructions

1. *Cut shapes from craft foam:* Cut hat from black, two holly leaves from green, scarf A and scarf B from red; fringe end of scarf B. Using pinking shears, cut snowman from white; cut slashes for arms using scissors.

2. Paint cheeks pink; let dry. Paint wooden teardrop with two coats pumpkin, letting paint dry between coats.

3. Using fine-tip marker, draw mouth line and outline cheeks; outline carrot nose and add detail lines; outline and add veins to holly leaves; outline both scarf pieces and add details to fringe.

4. Using paintbrush handle dipped in paints, dot on black spots along mouth line; add white and green dots to scarf pieces.

5. Thread full strand of white embroidery floss through holes in ⁷⁄₁₆" black buttons; knot floss on backs of buttons and trim away excess floss.

6. Using washable glue, glue gingham ribbon across hat; glue ⁷⁄₁₆" buttons onto face for eyes and ⁹⁄₁₆" buttons down front of snowman's body.

7. Using foam glue, glue holly leaves to hat; glue red

Snowman
Cut 1 from white craft foam using pinking shears

button over ends of leaves. Glue hat onto snowman. Glue pumpkin nose and scarf pieces in place.

8. *Hanger:* Fold gold ribbon in half; glue cut ends to back of hat.

9. Insert candy canes in slits as shown; secure on wrong side of snowman with tape. ❈

Holly Leaf
Cut 2 from green craft foam

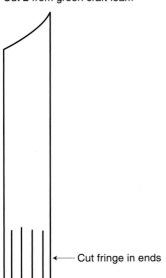

← Cut fringe in ends

Scarf B
Cut 1 from red craft foam

Hat
Cut 1 from black craft foam

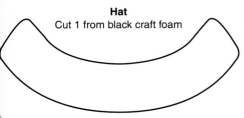

Scarf A
Cut 1 from red craft foam

Holiday Hospitality

Welcome friends, family and other loved ones into your holiday home this Christmas season! To make your entertaining a success from start to finish, you'll love crafting table sets and accents, place cards, floral centerpieces and much more!

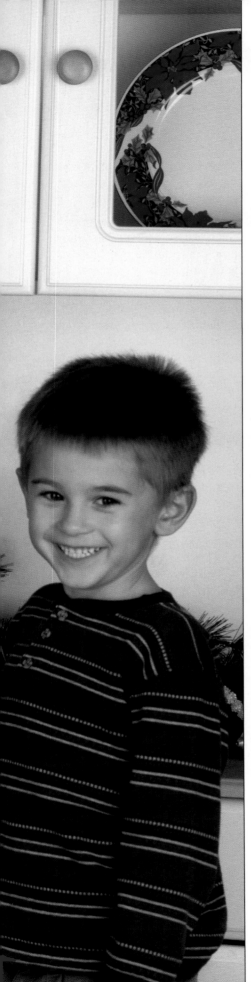

Candyland Christmas Tree

Frosted with sugar and sparkling with candy treats of all kinds, this fanciful creation will leave you with visions of sugarplums!

Design by Lori Blankenship

Materials

- Plastic foam tree*
- Assorted miniature imitation candy ornaments, individually packaged or cut from packaged garlands (see Project Notes)
- 2 (5") flat imitation lollipops
- Adhesive*
- Hunter green spray stain*
- Crystal glitter
- Snow writer*
- Ruby glitter fabric paint*
- Small, fine-tip squeeze bottle
- 26-gauge wire
- Needle-nose wire cutters
- Old paintbrush
- 8" ⅛"-wide gold-edge white satin ribbon

Styrofoam plastic-foam Stak Tree from Dow Chemical Company; The Ultimate Adhesive from API Crafter's Pick; Design Master Colortool Spray stain; and Scribbles Snow Writer and Ultra Glitter fabric paint from Duncan.

Project Notes

Refer to photo throughout.

Follow manufacturers' instructions for applying spray and assembling tree.

In addition to the lollipops on top of tree, imitation candies used on sample project (from top down) include strings of multicolored ring-shaped candies, acrylic multi-colored "frosted" wrapped ball candies, peppermint half-balls, 2" lollipops in assorted colors, 2¼" candy canes and assorted 1" "frosted" heart-shaped candies.

Instructions

1. Using old paintbrush, coat exterior of each section of tree with adhesive; let dry.

2. Spray each section with spray stain; let dry.

3. Assemble tree. Apply a second coat of stain. Load squeeze bottle with crystal glitter and "spritz" onto tree while stain is still wet. Let dry.

4. Cut 40 (1½") pieces of wire; using tip of wire cutters as a mold, shape each piece into a staple; set aside.

5. Assemble and prepare "candies," removing them from garlands, trimming off hangers, cutting them in half, etc., as needed.

6. Using wire staples (step 4) and adhesive, attach candies to "layers" of tree. On sections without candy, decorate with squiggles or swags of snow paint or glitter paint.

7. Cross sticks of larger lollipops and wire together; secure lollipops to top of tree with wire staple and adhesive. Tie ribbon in a bow; glue to lollipops to conceal wire. ❈

Snowmen Mugs

Warm your guests' hearts with the cute snowmen on these mugs.

Designs by Shelia Sommers

Materials

- Large ceramic mug
- Enamel air-dry paints*: chocolate, tangerine, cotton candy pink, classic navy blue, crocus yellow, ultra white, tropical purple, ultra black, 14K gold, eggplant, chili pepper, shiny emerald green
- Surface conditioner*
- Clear gloss glaze*
- Thinner*
- Paintbrushes: ¼" angular, 10/0 liner, #14 flat, and beat-up, scruffy #5 flat
- Sponge
- Toothbrush
- Snow Friends and Snowflakes pre-cut stencils*

*Ceramcoat PermEnamel Air-Dry and emerald green Shimmers Air-Dry Paint, surface conditioner, clear gloss glaze, thinner/dilutant and Stencil Magic Holiday Pre-Cut stencils, all from Delta.

Project Notes

Refer to photo throughout.

Ceramic mugs used for sample projects are 4½" tall and 3½" in diameter.

Read through all Project Notes, "Working With PermEnamel Paints" and instructions before beginning.

Refer to directions for Base-coating, Shading, Highlighting and Stenciling with Sponges under "Painting Techniques" in the General Instructions, page 190.

Working With PermEnamel Paints

PermEnamel paints are a polyester-based product designed for application on glass, tile and ceramic surfaces. Do not mix with other brands of enamel paints. PermEnamel paints require only air drying—no heat-setting is needed.

It is important to let projects cure for about 10 days after painting before washing. Once cured, projects are dishwasher safe, and microwave- and oven-proof.

Base coat should be applied after surface conditioner has dried but within four hours of its application. If you wait longer, bonding agents in the conditioner will have evaporated, requiring application of another coat of surface conditioner before you proceed.

It is *very important* to let all coats of paint dry before adding the next coat. Do not use a blow dryer to speed the drying process; heat can cause the bonding agents in the conditioner to evaporate.

Substitute Delta Thinner/Dilutant for water when diluting PermEnamel paints for shading or highlighting; water breaks down the bonding agents in the paints.

Preparation

1. Thoroughly clean mug with soap and water before painting. Rinse completely to remove any residues, then dry with a clean, lint-free towel.

2. Apply a coat of surface conditioner to surface to be painted; let air-dry.

3. When conditioner is dry and within four hours of applying surface conditioner, base-coat exterior of mug with purple, omitting handle and bringing color up to but not over or onto the lip of the mug. Apply a second coat after paint has dried completely.

Painting

1. *Snowman with star:* Holding stencil on one side of mug, paint design as follows, allowing paints to air-dry as needed between applications:

Hat: Sponge with chili pepper; shade with eggplant; dab yellow onto pompom on tip of hat; shade with tangerine.

Snowman: Pour puddle of white onto palette. Dip bristles of beat-up #5 flat brush into paint and dab onto palette, removing excess while blending color across bristles. Using a very light touch, dab paint onto pre-cut design for snowman. When dry, shade snowman with navy blue. Dot on eyes and mouth using tip of paintbrush handle dipped in black; add black eyelashes with liner brush and dot a white highlight dot onto each eye. Paint nose with tangerine and heart-shaped cheek with pink.

Scarf: Sponge stripes at ends of scarf with chili pepper; sponge remaining stripes in an alternating pattern of yellow and chili pepper. Shade bottom edges of yellow stripes with tangerine and bottom edges of chili pepper stripes with eggplant. Using liner, add yellow fringe at ends of scarf.

Star: Sponge with yellow; shade with tangerine.

2. *Snowman with coat:* Holding stencil on other side of mug, paint design as follows:

Hat: Sponge stocking portion and pompom on end with green; sponge hat brim with chili pepper; shade with eggplant and use liner to add thin crocus yellow stripes.

Snowman: Paint as for snowman with star, omitting cheeks.

Scarf: Sponge with chili pepper;

shade with eggplant. Using liner and yellow, add thin stripes across scarf and fringe at ends.

Christmas tree: Paint tree green and trunk chocolate.

Coat and mittens: Sponge coat with navy blue. Sponge heart and mittens with chili pepper and shade with eggplant. Paint buttons with gold.

3. *Snowflakes:* Using white and snowflake stencil, sponge snowflakes randomly over surface of mug between and around snowmen. Using end of paintbrush handle dipped in white, add several large dots.

4. Load bristles of toothbrush with white and lightly spatter painted surface of mug.

5. When paint is *completely* dry, apply glaze to painted design. ❄

Grapevine Wreaths

Make these charming wreaths as napkin holders to add a festive touch to your Christmas dinner. Add the candle trimmers as an accent to your centerpiece.

Designs by Dorothy Egan

Materials
Each Napkin Ring & Candle Trimmer

- Grapevine wreaths: 2" for candle trimmers, 3" for napkin rings
- 24" ⅛"- to ⅜"-wide ribbon (see Instructions for individual designs)
- Metallic gold spray paint (see Project Notes)
- Glorious gold metallic paint*
- Fine craft wire
- Dried and silk botanicals, floral picks, ribbons and other materials as desired (see Instructions for individual designs)
- Hot-glue gun

*Dazzling Metallics acrylic paint from Delta.

Continued on page 139

Wired Basket

Transform a discount-store container into a stylish tote, then pile it high with homemade treats, soaps and bath beads, or a pair of mugs filled with coffees and teas.

Design by Joan Fee

Materials

- Wire basket
- 20-gauge silver-plated copper wire in assorted colors*
- Wire worker*
- Assorted beads and/or charms
- Round-nose pliers
- Wire cutters

Wire and Twist 'n Curl wire worker from Artistic Wire.

Project Note

Refer to photo throughout.

Instructions

1. Wrap wire randomly through basket, securing ends around basket and adding beads where desired.

2. *Dangles:* Assemble wire worker by screwing desired bar into hole at center of handle. Cut 6" piece of wire; insert one end into hole in handle and wrap around base. Wrap wire around bar, holding it in place with your fingers and leaving about 1" uncurled at end. Slip coil off bar; wrap dangle around wire on basket using round-nose pliers. Repeat to make desired number of bangles.

3. *Handle:* Wrap handle with wire as desired, securing wire ends at base of handle. ❈

Christmas Tree Apron

Bring your Christmas tree into the kitchen with this fun and colorful apron.
Make one for each of the kids to wear when helping you bake Christmas cookies!

Design by Mary Ayres

Materials

- Green apron*
- 3 yards metallic gold jumbo rickrack
- Cotton fabrics: ¼ yard gold; scraps of purple, pink, red, orange and blue
- Needled cotton batting*
- Sewing machine (optional)
- Hand-sewing needle and matching threads

Apron from Innovo Inc.; and Warm & Natural batting from The Warm Company.

Project Notes

Refer to pattern and photo throughout.

To transfer pattern, refer to instructions for "Using Transfer & Graphite Paper" in the General Instructions, page 190.

Instructions

1. Wash and dry apron without using fabric softener; press as needed.

2. Cut two stars from gold fabric and one from cotton batting. Baste batting to wrong side of one fabric star; on right side of same star, sew rickrack ¼" from edge, beginning and ending in a corner and stitching down the center of the rickrack.

3. Lay second fabric star atop the first right sides facing and sew all layers together, leaving a 3" opening along bottom for turning, and stitching on top of the stitching used to attach rickrack. Turn star right side out; sew opening closed with needle and thread. Attach star to center top of apron using invisible stitches.

4. Using yellow thread and invisible stitches, sew rickrack garland to apron front, beginning at top right and turning under raw edge of rickrack; drape rickrack from side to side, folding it back toward front at each edge. Turn raw edge under in back on bottom right.

5. *Yo-yo ornaments:* Cut two 4" circles from each of the remaining fabrics. Turn under raw edge of one circle ⅛"; sew basting stitch around edge. Pull stitches to gather circle and knot thread ends. Press yo-yo flat with gathered edge at center back. Repeat with remaining circles.

6. Using invisible stitches, sew yo-yos to apron with gathered edges up. ❈

Tree Apron Star
Cut 2 from gold fabric and 1 from cotton batting

"Tea for Two" Apron

After the Christmas rush is over, treat yourself and a friend to a relaxing afternoon of hot tea and cookies. Wearing this painted apron will make the preparation as much fun as the relaxation.

Design by June Fiechter

Materials

- Royal blue apron*
- Fabric glue*
- Snowflake stencil*
- Pearl finish dimensional paints*: snow white, glacier blue
- Pearl finish fabric paints*: espresso, gun metal
- #4 round fabric-painting brush
- 10" ⅞"-wide sheer metallic silver ribbon
- Razor knife
- Cutting board
- Transfer paper

Apron #0151 from BagWorks; Aleene's No-Sew Fabric Glue, Tulip's Design Your Own #SL012 Stick-Ease Stencil, Pearl Dimensional and Pearl Fabric paints, all from Duncan.

Project Notes

Refer to photo, patterns and stencil diagram throughout.

To transfer patterns, refer to instructions for "Using Transfer & Graphite Paper" in the General Instructions on page 190.

Use photocopier to enlarge patterns 125 percent before transferring.

Let all paints dry between applications.

Cups & Saucers

1. Wash and dry apron without using fabric softener; press as needed.

2. Transfer cup-and-saucer pattern onto stencil using transfer paper. Cut out using razor knife and cutting board.

3. Place stencil on front of apron, positioning with regard to placement of second cup and saucer.

4. Using fabric-painting brush, paint cup and saucer glacier blue, and contents of cup espresso. Let dry completely.

5. Remove stencil; reposition for second motif, reversing handle position. Paint as in step 4.

6. Outline cups and saucers with white dimensional paint, holding tip of bottle against fabric at a slight angle so that only a small amount of paint flows onto fabric.

7. Using same method and applying paint directly from bottle, add detail lines to saucers with blue.

8. Transfer remaining details as needed; using white applied directly from the bottle, add snowflake to each cup and handles to cups. Using gun metal, add steam rising from cups.

Apron Trim

1. *Top edge of apron:* Dollop white paint over top band of edge-binding tape. Apply blue from bottle in scalloped pattern just below white binding. Add row of white dots under scallops.

2. *Pocket:* Repeat step 1 across top of pocket. When completely dry, tie ribbon in a simple bow; trim ends and glue to edge of pocket. ❄

Placement Diagram
Enlarge 125% before transferring

Stencil Pattern
Enlarge 125% before transferring

Snowflakes

Frosty Gel Candle

Add a glow of festive fun to your home all winter long with this fun-to-paint candle!

Design by Mary Ayres

Materials

- 3" round clear glass candle holder
- 16 assorted flat white buttons
- 8 ounces aquamarine candle gel*
- Gel-candle iridescent glitter*
- Enamel air-dry paints*: cotton candy pink, ultra white, ultra black, frosted orange slice
- 6" gel-candle wick*
- Plastic circular template with 2¼", ¾" and ½" circles
- Tweezers
- Round bristle brush

Candle gel, Gel Candles Special Effects Iridescent Glitter, Ceramcoat PermEnamel Air-Dry and Frosted Looks paints, and Gel Candles wick, all from Delta.

Project Notes

Refer to photo throughout.

Follow manufacturer's instructions for using gel candle products.

Before beginning, refer to directions for "Working With PermEnamel Paints" included with Project Notes for "Snowman Mugs," page 124.

Candle

1. Melt candle gel. Sprinkle a small amount of glitter into melted gel; stir.

2. Using tweezers, dip each button into melted gel and press it in position on inside of candle holder, placing buttons randomly around sides and leaving a blank 2½"-wide area on one side where face can be added later. Anchor wick in candle holder; secure top end around pencil.

3. Pour melted gel into candle holder to within ¼" of top; let cool. Trim wick ¼" above surface of gel.

Painting

1. Using template, position 2¼" circle on blank side of candle holder. Brush one coat of white paint onto circle on candle holder using a dabbing motion.

2. Using template, position ½" circle in center of white circle for nose; brush with two coats orange for nose, using a dabbing motion.

3. Using template, position ¾" circle off to one side of nose for cheek; brush with one coat pink, using a dabbing motion. When dry, repeat for second cheek.

4. Applying black paint with the end of the paintbrush handle, dot on two eyes centered above nose, and seven dots centered under nose for mouth.

5. Applying white paint with the end of a smaller paintbrush handle, dot a single highlight onto each cheek. ❋

Gumdrop Favors

*Share "visions of sugarplums" with holiday guests when you
enhance your table with these festive favors "frosted" with glitter!*

Design by Kathi Taylor Shearer

Materials
Each Favor

- 2" clear plastic champagne glass or compote
- Fine white/iridescent glitter
- 10" circle fine white tulle
- 3"–4" iridescent floral spray with beads, pearls or sequins
- ¾ yard ¼"-wide iridescent poly ribbon
- ⅓ yard small iridescent pearls-on-a-string
- 8" white cloth-covered wire
- 7–9 small sugared gumdrops in assorted colors
- Small disposable paintbrush
- Tacky craft glue

Project Note

Refer to photo throughout.

Instructions

1. Using disposable brush, coat exterior surfaces of champagne glass with glue. Shake glitter over wet glue and let dry completely. Tap off excess glitter.

2. Form single-loop "shoelace" bow from pearls; secure center with wire but do not trim wire ends.

3. Form triple-loop bow from ribbon; position pearl bow over center and secure with wire; do not trim ends.

4. Fill glass with gumdrops.

5. Fold tulle circle in half; cut 1½" slit in center of fold. Slip base of glass through slit; gather tulle circle up around glass and gumdrops, inserting bottom of floral spray between gathers. Secure gathered tulle and floral spray with ends of wires used to secure bows. Trim wire ends; trim ends of ribbon as desired. ❈

Holiday Tablecloth

*Deck your table in sweet fashion with a covering boasting
a whole jarful of tasty gingerbread cookies and other treats.*

Design by Shelia Sommers

Materials

- 60" x 82" light blue tablecloth
- Fabrics: 1⅔ yards light-colored; ½ yard light brown; ¼ yard each red print and white print; scraps of purple print
- Sewing threads: light blue to match tablecloth; white; light brown, red and purple to match fabrics
- Embroidery floss: dark brown, black
- Gold metallic embroidery floss or thread
- Needles: hand-sewing and embroidery
- Straight pins
- Sewing machine with zigzag stitch
- Fabric colors*: starlite white, peppermint
- Snowflakes holiday stencil*
- Stencil sponge*
- Fabric glue*
- 70 small black seed beads
- 36 round white pearl beads
- Fusible web*
- White baby rickrack
- Cotton-tipped swabs
- Transfer paper
- Iron

Starlite Shimmering Fabric Colors, Stencil Magic holiday stencil, stencil sponge and Stitchless Glue from Delta, and Wonder Under fusible web.

Project Notes

Refer to photo and patterns throughout.

Pattern repeat: On sample, pattern—including three gingerbread men, a peppermint, a peppermint stick and a wrapped candy—repeats every 18".

Adjust spacing and amounts of materials if you use a tablecloth of a different size.

To transfer patterns, refer to instructions for "Using Transfer & Graphite Paper" in the General Instructions, page 190.

Follow manufacturer's instructions for using fusible web, stencil products and paints.

Cutting & Border Panels

1. Prewash and dry all fabrics and tablecloth without using fabric softener; press with iron.

2. Fuse fusible web to wrong side of white, red, purple and light brown fabrics.

3. Cut pieces from fused fabrics as follows: *light brown:* 11 gingerbread men A, 12 gingerbread men B and 12 gingerbread men C; *white:* 11 complete peppermint stick shapes and 12 complete peppermint rounds; *red:* corresponding stripes for peppermint sticks and rounds; *purple:* 12 "column" shapes for wrapped candies.

4. Using pencil, lightly sketch inner lines on gingerbread men, tips of peppermint sticks and wrapped candies; these will be used as guides later.

5. From light-colored border fabric, cut two strips 8½" x 60" and two strips 8½" x 66".

6. Pin cutouts onto strips of light-colored fabric, centering cutouts on strips and repeating pattern every 18" (see Project Notes). Fuse pieces to border fabric, adding red stripes to peppermints as you go.

7. Using sewing machine and

mouths, adding a French knot at each end of mouth. Using 2 strands black floss, attach black beads for eyes and add short, straight eyelashes.

4. Using sewing needle and white thread, sew a white bead to center of each peppermint round; sew two white beads for buttons down fronts of gingerbread men B and C.

5. Using embroidery needle and metallic gold floss, add straight stitches at ends of purple wrapped candies.

Assembly & Finishing

1. When all sewing and embroidery is complete, fuse fusible web

to wrong side of each border strip.

2. Turn under edges of border panels; press. Pin border panels around tablecloth 2" from edges. Using light blue thread, machine-stitch panels to tablecloth using short straight stitch and stitching ⅛" from folded edge.

3. Using stencil, stencil sponge and white paint, stencil snowflakes in center of tablecloth. (Practice first on a piece of dark paper or fabric.) Dot smaller "snowflakes" randomly between stenciled flakes using swab dipped in white. Let dry. ❄

matching threads, outline each piece and add inner lines with zigzag stitch.

Embroidery & Embellishments

1. Using paint and swab, dot cheeks onto each gingerbread man; let dry.

2. Cut baby rickrack to fit across gingerbread men's arms; dip ends in glue to prevent fraying. Let glue dry, then sew each piece in place by machine using white thread and straight stitch.

3. Using embroidery needle and 2 strands brown floss, embroider

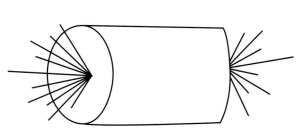

Wrapped Candy
Cut 12 candy shapes from
purple print

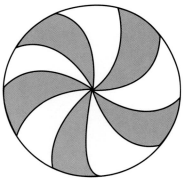

Peppermint Candy
Cut 12 complete rounds from white;
cut stripes from red

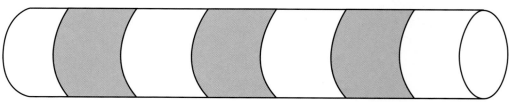

Peppermint Stick
Cut 11 complete shapes from white;
cut stripes from red

Gingerbread Man A
Cut 11 from light brown

Gingerbread Man B
Cut 12 from light brown

Gingerbread Man C
Cut 12 from light brown

Snowy Pine Table Runner

*Dress up your table or sideboard with this woodsy table
runner enhanced by stitched ribbon snowflakes.*

Design by Mary T. Cosgrove

Materials

- Twill natural table runner*
- Rambling pine pre-cut stencil*
- Repositionable stencil spray*
- Fabric color*: brown, light beige, brownstone, hunter green
- White brush-on fabric color*
- Stencil brushes or stencil sponges
- Brush cleaner*
- 7 yards 4mm white silk embroidery ribbon*
- Chenille needle
- Iron

*Table runner #4254 from BagWorks; Stencil Magic Pre-Cut Decorative Stencil #95-183-0018, Stencil Magic Repositionable Stencil Spray, Starlite Shimmering Fabric Color, Fabric Dye BrushOn Fabric Color and Ceramcoat brush cleaner, all from Delta; and ribbon from Bucilla.

Japanese Ribbon Stitch

Project Notes

Refer to photo and Figs. 1 and 2 throughout.

Refer to manufacturer's instructions for using stenciling products.

Refer to directions for stenciling under "Painting Techniques" in General Instructions, page 190.

Instructions

1. Spray back of stencil with stencil adhesive; wait until adhesive is tacky before proceeding.

2. Lay table runner flat on protected work surface. Using desired size brush and/or sponge, stencil entire pattern on left end of runner as follows: *beige:* bottoms of pinecones where they attach to branch; *brown:* remainder of pinecones; *brownstone:* tree branch; *hunter green:* pine needles.

3. In center of runner, stencil left side of pattern up to the fourth pinecone; then repeat entire stencil to finish. Let dry; clean brushes and stencil.

4. Add touches of "snow" to limbs, pinecones and pine needles with white paint. Let dry.

5. *Referring to diagram for Japanese ribbon stitch, add embroidered snowflakes randomly to surface of table runner:* Cut an 18" length of ribbon for each snowflake. Thread one end onto chenille needle; pierce that end with point of needle about ½" from end, and pull tail to secure ribbon in needle. First stitch four longer stitches (1–2, 3–4, 5–6 and 7–8), bringing needle up from back of fabric, laying ribbon flat, and then piercing through center of ribbon and fabric ¾"–1" from starting point. Add shorter diagonal stitches (9–10, 11–12, 13–14 and 15–16), making them ½" in length. When you reach other end of ribbon, make a running stitch and pull needle through to knot end.

6. Iron wrong side of runner to heat-set paint. Follow paint manufacturer's instructions for laundering. ✳

Grapevine Wreaths

Continued from page 126

Project Notes

Refer to photo throughout.

As an alternative to spraying botanicals with gold paint, use gilded floral picks, dried botanicals, etc.

Adapt designs as desired to use the botanicals and other supplies you have on hand.

Instructions

1. Spray botanicals and other materials with spray paint as desired; let dry completely.

2. Begin by gluing a base of greenery to the wreath. If using ribbon, tie a four-loop bow and tie it tightly in the center with wire. Wire bow and spot-glue over center of greenery.

3. Add additional trims over and around bow as desired:

Gold berries and white roses: To a base of greenery, add a bow of ⅛"-wide white/gold ribbon; finish with small gold twigs, gold blackberries, small white roses with leaves and dried white "button" flowers.

Gold-tipped pinecone wreath: To a base of greenery, add a bow of ¼"-wide gold ribbon; finish with small gold twigs, small pinecones and greenery with small gold berries.

Crabapple wreath: To a base of greenery, add a bow of ⅜"-wide burgundy ribbon; finish with sprigs of gold-sprayed eucalyptus, assorted crabapples and berries.

Flocked poinsettia wreath: To a base of greenery, add a 1½"–2" flocked poinsettia and finish with an assortment of red and green berries and small gold twigs.

4. Insert napkins in napkin rings; place candle trimmers around base of taper candles. Remove before lighting candles. ✳

Wreath Coasters

Keep your coffee table free from glass rings while adding a festive holiday touch with this coaster set. The wreaths are so pretty you won't want to cover them up with glasses!

Design by June Fiechter

Materials

- Craft canvas*: 15" x 2½" strip, 4¾" circle, 4 (4") circles
- Kelly green felt*
- Acrylic paints*: linen, olive green, mushroom, Victorian rose, rose garden, clover, English mustard
- Decoupage medium*
- Paintbrushes*
- 24" magenta raffia ribbon*
- Fabric adhesive*
- Scallop-edge scissors*
- Graphite paper
- Shredded natural raffia or excelsior (optional)

Kreative Kanvas and felt from Kunin; FolkArt acrylic paints, Outdoor Mod Podge decoupage medium, Paintbrush Set #41055 and Raffia Accents Ribbon, all from Plaid; Fabri-Tac adhsive from Beacon; and Fiskars scallop-edge scissors.

Project Notes

To transfer patterns, refer to instructions for "Using Transfer & Graphite Paper" in the General Instructions, page 190.

Let all paints and decoupage medium dry between applications.

Coasters

1. Trim edges of all 4" circles with scallop-edge scissors.

2. Transfer pattern of inner circle and bow to center of all four coasters; do not transfer clusters of dots.

3. Paint fronts of coasters as follows: *olive green:* wreaths; *rose garden:* bow; *mustard:* center circle.

4. Highlight bow with Victorian rose; shade center circle with mushroom.

5. *Add dimension to wreaths:* Dip stencil brush into clover; dab excess paint off onto paper towel. "Pounce" brush onto olive green portions, avoiding outer ¼" and inner ⅛" of wreath.

6. Repeat step 5 substituting linen paint for clover.

7. *Dot "berries" onto wreath:* Dip handle of largest paintbrush into mustard; dot on clusters of dots. Dip handle of smallest brush into linen; dot highlight onto each mustard dot.

8. Coat painted surface of coasters with decoupage medium.

9. *Felt backing:* Cut a circle of felt to fit back of each coaster, making sure no felt is visible from front. Glue felt backing in place.

Holder

1. Trim one long edge of the 15" x 2½" canvas strip (sides) with scalloped scissors.

2. Using regular scissors, cut the other long edge in a pattern of evenly spaced, ½"-deep, V-shaped notches.

3. Paint both sides of 15" x 2½" strip and 4¾" circle (base) with olive green.

4. Add dimension to outside of strip as directed in steps 5 and 6 for coasters, applying paints all the way to scalloped edge and avoiding notches and ⅜"-wide strip adjacent to notches.

5. Dot "berries" onto outside of strip as in step 7 for coasters, applying clusters randomly to surface of strip.

Wreath Coaster

6. *Assemble holder:* Bend strip around canvas circle and, working with four notches at a time, apply glue to their inside surface and affix them to outer surface of 4¾" base circle. Allow glue to dry before gluing next four notches. Repeat process around holder until all notches are glued to bottom of base and ends of strip meet; bond ends with glue.

7. Paint all surfaces of holder with a coat of decoupage medium.

8. Cut a circle of felt to fit bottom of holder.

9. Wrap raffia around sides of holder and tie in a bow, fanning out bow loops. Tack in place with dots of glue.

10. Place a small "nest" of shredded natural raffia or excelsior in bottom of holder, if desired; place coasters in holder. ❈

Sweet Treats

Never one to miss out on a treat, this little holiday visitor helps himself to a festive snack.

Design by Jackie Haskell

Materials

- Polymer clay*: white, black, yellow, red, dusty rose, turquoise
- 2 black seed beads
- Sparkle glaze*
- Small paintbrush
- Straight-edge tool
- Straight pin
- Clean white rag or fabric napkin
- Oven-proof plate
- Oven

Sculpey III polymer clay and sparkle glaze from Delta.

Project Notes

Refer to photo throughout.

Clean all traces of color from fingers with white rag or napkin before working with next color.

Use a pin to remove any pieces of lint or fibers that stick to the clay, then smooth clay with fingers to remove pin marks.

Instructions

1. *Body:* Blend ⅓ of a brick of black clay with ⅔ brick of white clay to make gray. Knead and blend thoroughly with your fingers until clay is an even gray color with no visible streaks of white or black. Cut a quarter-section from this brick of gray clay, then cut it into four equal pieces. Roll one piece into a ball and form it into a teardrop.

2. *Arms:* Form two pea-size balls of gray, one for each arm. Form each into a ¾" cone; attach smaller ends to pointed part of body. Slightly flatten and round other ends to form paws.

3. *Head:* Shape a marble-size ball of gray into a slight teardrop shape. Turn up pointed end of teardrop to form nose. Push beads on edge into the face for eyes until none of bead hole is visible. Using pin, indent two eyelashes at outer corners of eyes, and add short, straight eyebrows; add vertical line down from tip of nose. Roll a very tiny ball of rose; attach to tip of nose above line. Gently press head onto body.

4. *Feet:* Roll marble-size ball of gray; cut in half and shape each into a teardrop. Attach to body with tops of feet—rounded edges—pointing outward. Roll two small balls of rose; flatten each into a teardrop shape and press into place on bottoms of feet, points down.

5. *Ears:* Cut a pea-size ball of gray in half. Slightly flatten each piece into a circle; attach to head. Roll two tiny balls of rose; flatten and attach to ears for ear centers.

6. *Tail:* Form a pea-size ball of gray into a 2" rope; set aside.

7. *Peppermint candy:* Roll three half-marble-size pieces red and three half-marble-size pieces white. Roll each into a ball, then shape each into a ¾" teardrop. Place pointed ends of teardrops together, alternating colors; set peppermint on its side and carefully roll along table to create flat edge. When edges are flat and teardrops are firmly attached, lay peppermint flat on table and continue shaping as needed.

8. *Gumdrops:* Roll a marble-size ball each of turquoise, rose and yellow; shape each into a gumdrop with flat bottom.

9. *Assembly:* Attach one end of mouse's tail to back of body; firmly but carefully, set mouse on peppermint candy. Bring tail around to right side and attach to candy. Place turquoise gumdrop in mouse's arms. Attach other gumdrops to edge of peppermint, one standing up and one on its side.

10. *Baking:* Place piece on oven-proof plate; bake in preheated 275-degree oven for 10 minutes. Let cool completely.

11. Paint gumdrops and peppermint with glaze. ❉

Christmas Goodies

A brimming cookie jar is one of the sweet gifts of Christmas!
Sculpt this delightful image and attach to a magnet.

Design by Jackie Haskell

Materials

- Polymer clay*: white, green, yellow, red, tan, dusty rose, lavender, ivory brilliant, turquoise
- 2 black seed beads
- Straight-edge tool
- Straight pin
- Small star punch tool for clay
- Clean white rag or fabric napkin
- Oven-proof plate
- Oven
- ½" button magnet
- Hot-glue gun

Sculpey III polymer clay.

Project Notes

Refer to photo throughout.

Clean all traces of color from fingers with white rag or napkin before working with next color.

Use a pin to remove any pieces of lint or fibers that stick to the clay, then smooth clay with fingers to remove pin marks.

Jar

1. *Jar:* Cut a quarter-section from brick of ivory compound, then cut that piece in half. Soften one half and roll it into a ball. Working on a flat surface to keep back flat, form ball into jar by flattening it into a circle. Flatten bottom edge of jar on work surface and form a slight indentation in top edge where goodies will be positioned.

2. *Lid:* Roll marble-size ball of ivory compound; form into an elongated half-circle, working on a flat surface to keep back flat.

3. *Jar trim:* From a pea-size ball of green, form a 7½" rope. Attach rope to lid and jar and cut as needed with scissors. Press rope lightly to flatten it. Cut ⅛ from another pea-size ball of green; roll this tiny piece into a ball for lid handle and press onto lid.

Gingerbread Man

1. *Head:* Slightly flatten a pea-size ball of tan into a circle; push beads on their edges into the face for eyes until none of bead hole is visible. Roll a very tiny ball of tan for nose; attach to face. Using pin, indent two eyelashes at outer corner of eyes, and add eyebrows and smile. Roll two identical, tiny balls of rose; press onto ends of smile for cheeks.

2. *Arms:* Use quarter-pea-size ball of tan for each arm; form each into ½" cone. Attach smaller ends of cones under head; slightly flatten and round off other ends for hands.

Stars & Candies

1. *Stars:* Roll pea-size ball of yellow; flatten evenly. Using star punch tool, punch three stars.

2. *Candy canes:* Roll a quarter-pea-size ball each of red and white; shape each into a 1¾" rope. Twist ropes together; cut resulting twisted rope in half and round off ends. Curve end of each to make two candy canes.

3. *Ribbon candies:* Cut a pea-size ball of turquoise into eight identical pieces; use two of these pieces for ribbon candies. Form each into

a ½" rope; flatten. Fold each to make two pieces of ribbon candy.

4. *Lollipop:* Use quarter-pea-size balls each of lavender and dusty rose. Form each into a 1¼" rope, then twist ropes together as for candy canes. Coil twisted rope around itself to make a flat circle. For stick, cut off ⅛ from a pea-size ball of white and form it into a ½" stick shape; attach to lollipop.

Assembly & Finishing

1. *Assembly:* Position gingerbread man on top edge of jar with left hand holding one star and right hand attached to jar. Attach candy canes, lollipop, remaining stars and ribbon candies to jar as shown. Attach lid at an angle against jar and gingerbread man's head.

2. *Baking:* Place piece on oven-proof plate; bake in preheated 275-degree oven for 10 minutes. Let cool completely.

3. Hot-glue magnet to back of cookie jar. ❈

Holiday Dinnerware

Serve your Christmas dinner on this festive, painted set covered with Santas and snowflakes!
Make enough dishes for the whole family to enjoy.

Designs by Bev Shenefield

Materials
- Green dishware*: dinner plate, salad plate, latte mug, Asian coupe bowl, transparent acrylic 16-ounce tumbler
- Gloss acrylic enamel paints*: gloss white, gloss black, Christmas red, rose mauve
- Paintbrushes: #8 flat, #1 spotter, #20/0 script liner
- Vinegar
- Expandable sponge
- Pointed wooden skewer

Series 0041 dishware from Zakware; and Ultra Gloss acrylic enamel paints from DecoArt.

Project Notes
Refer to photo and patterns throughout.

Refer to manufacturer's instructions for using paints before beginning.

Santa

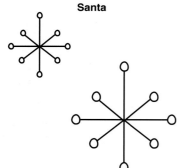

Snowflakes

Let all paints dry between applications.

Let painted pieces air-dry for at least seven days before washing; do not soak. *To make painted dishware dishwasher safe:* Wait for at least 24 hours after painting, then bake pieces in a preheated 325-degree oven for 30 minutes.

Instructions

1. Wash all dishware with vinegar to remove all oils and residues; rinse thoroughly with water and let air-dry or dry with lint-free cloth.

2. Cut Santa shape from expandable sponge; expand sponge in water and wring out.

3. Using flat brush, paint one side of Santa sponge completely with red. Press sponge onto dishware; light pressure will make thinner Santas, while heavier pressure will make fatter Santas. Space Santas evenly around dishware; on samples, dinner plates and salad plates have eight Santas, latte mugs have three (handle occupies position where fourth Santa would be placed), and tumblers and bowls have four.

4. Using spotter brush and a mixture of mauve and white, paint face areas on Santas.

5. Using flat brush, pat additional red onto hat and suit areas. Touch up as needed once paint has dried.

6. Using spotter brush and black, paint boots and gloves.

7. Using spotter brush and white, dab on beards, fur trim on suits at wrists, legs and belt lines, and pom-poms on tips of hats.

8. Using tip of skewer dipped in black, dot on eyes.

9. Using liner and white, paint single snowflakes evenly spaced between Santas, using smaller snowflakes on tumblers and larger snowflakes on other pieces. Using brush handle dipped in white, dot ends of vertical and horizontal arms of snowflakes; use skewer dipped in white to add dots at ends of shorter diagonal arms. ❄

Holly Burner Covers

These painted burner covers will add a yuletide touch to an area usually overlooked during holiday decorating.

Design by Bev Shenefield

Materials

- 2 small and 2 large green metal burner covers
- Metal paints*: real red, true green, bright lime green, coal black
- Paintbrushes: #1 spotter, #20/0 liner
- Vinegar

No-Prep Metal Paints from DecoArt.

Project Note

Refer to pattern and photo throughout, or paint holly clusters freehand.

Instructions

1. Wash burner covers with vinegar to remove any oils or other residue; let dry thoroughly.

2. *Paint holly leaves in clusters of three around edge of burner cover:* Begin leaves using spotter brush and lime green; add true green to give leaves a variegated look. When first border is complete, add a second row above the first, spacing clusters of holly leaves randomly to give a "scalloped" appearance. Let paints dry.

3. Using liner brush and a mixture of true green and black, add vein down center of each holly leaf; let dry.

4. Using paintbrush handle dipped in red, dot three or four berries in center of each cluster of leaves; let dry. ❈

Holly Burner Covers

Christmas Candle

Rub-ons make decorating the candle of your choice so simple that you will want to make several for yourself and to give away as gifts. Make a set in different colors, designs, scents and sizes!

Design by Marlene Watson

Materials
- Pillar candle in desired color and size
- Metallic gold snowflake rub-on transfers*
- Crystal glitter paint*
- Rubbing alcohol
- Soft, lint-free cloth
- Wooden craft stick

*Precious Metals Rub-On Art Transfers #PM218M from ChartPak; and Craft Twinkles paint from DecoArt.

Project Notes

Refer to photo throughout.

Refer to manufacturer's instructions for using rub-on transfers.

Instructions

1. Using soft cloth, clean surface of candle with rubbing alcohol and dry thoroughly.

2. Leaving tissue backing in place, cut transfer images apart (it is easier to work with one image at a time).

3. Remove tissue backing; position transfer on candle. Rub with craft stick, lifting one corner of cover sheet as you rub. Work your way across the design until carrier sheet is released; discard carrier sheet.

4. Wipe transfer with tissue backing to smooth it perfectly to the surface.

5. Repeat with remaining transfers, positioning them as desired.

6. Paint entire surface of candle with glitter paint, painting over transfers. Let dry completely. ❈

Christmas Vase & Frame

Glittering poinsettias star on this pair of elegant, mosaic-style accents for your holiday home.

Designs by Barbara Woolley

Materials

Each Project
- Ivory mosaic grout*
- Mosaic silicone adhesive*
- Old bowl and spoon for mixing grout
- Sponge
- Rubber gloves (optional)

Vase
- 5¼" sandstone rose bowl*
- 1 package alabaster marbleized acrylic pieces*
- 19mm x 10.5mm acrylic holly leaves*: 24 emerald green, 56 ruby
- 56 crystal 4mm acrylic faceted stones*

Frame
- 3" square unglazed ceramic frame
- 40–50 alabaster marbleized acrylic pieces*
- 19mm x 10.5mm acrylic holly leaves*: 4 emerald green, 6 ruby
- Acrylic faceted stones*: 10 (4mm) crystal, 3 (6mm) ruby
- Tweezers (optional)

Sandstone bowl from Syndicate Sales; Clearly Mosaics grout, adhesive and marbleized acrylic pieces #X272H, acrylic holly leaves (size #905) and faceted stones, all from The Beadery.

Project Notes
Refer to photo throughout.

Refer to manufacturer's instructions for using grout and adhesive.

Vase

1. Clean and dry surface of rose bowl.

2. Plan placement of eight poinsettias, positioned randomly on surface of rose bowl. Each poinsettia will require three green holly leaves for leaves, seven ruby holly leaves for petals, and seven crystal stones for center.

3. Using adhesive, glue three green leaves for first poinsettia around imaginary circle the size of a nickel, being sure to cover entire back of each leaf with adhesive. Wait a few minutes for adhesive to hold.

4. In same manner, glue four ruby leaves around same circle, gluing them over green leaves as necessary. Wait a few minutes for adhesive to hold.

5. Glue three remaining ruby leaves around circle, positioning them closer into the center and gluing them over the tops of the green and ruby leaves as necessary. Wait a few minutes for adhesive to hold.

6. Using tweezers if desired, glue seven crystal stones in a cluster in center of flower. There may be enough adhesive oozing from under petals and leaves to hold stones in place; add additional adhesive as needed.

7. Repeat steps 3–6 to add remaining poinsettias to bowl. Allow adhesive to set undisturbed for at least four hours before proceeding.

8. Covering back of each piece with adhesive, glue alabaster pieces over surface of bowl between poinsettias, fitting them together but allowing enough room between the pieces for adding grout later, mosaic-style. Let vase dry overnight.

9. Mix grout in bowl as directed. Press grout into spaces between alabaster "tiles" and between flowers, leaves and stones. Grout may lightly cover pieces.

10. Let grout set for 10 minutes, then remove excess grout with a damp sponge, gently rubbing surface in a circular motion. Let vase dry for 24 hours before handling.

Frame

Follow instructions as for vase, positioning a single poinsettia with two leaves and six petals (applied in two layers of three each) on top left corner of frame, and arrangement of two emerald holly leaves with ruby holly berries (faceted stones) on bottom right corner. ❀

Snowy Trivet & Coasters

Not looking forward to putting your Christmas gear away?
Keep the spirit alive for the remainder of winter with this painted table ensemble.

Designs by June Fiechter

Materials

- 7¾"-square white ceramic tile
- 4 (4¼"-square) white ceramic tiles
- Surface conditioner*
- Clear satin glaze*
- Enamel air-dry paints*: maize, country tomato, ultra black, dark goldenrod, midnight, pine green
- Paintbrushes
- Graphite paper
- Squares of white felt to fit the back of each ceramic tile
- Tacky craft glue
- Cotton-tip swab

Ceramcoat PermEnamel Air-Dry surface conditioner, clear satin glaze and paints from Delta.

Project Notes

Refer to photo and patterns throughout.

To transfer patterns, refer to instructions for "Using Transfer & Graphite Paper" in the General Instructions, page 190.

Follow manufacturer's instructions for using paints and other products.

Before beginning, refer to directions for "Working With PermEnamel Paints" included with Project Notes for "Snowman Mugs," page 124.

Let conditioner, paints and glaze dry between applications.

Instructions

1. Using transfer paper, transfer snowman design onto front of large tile and large snowflake onto center front of each small tile.

2. Apply surface conditioner to front of each tile. If transfer lines smear, wipe off with a cotton-tip swab.

3. Apply colors to tiles on front and edges; areas to be white should be left unpainted.

Coasters: Paint background of one coaster maize, one red, one midnight and one green.

Trivet: Paint as follows: *maize:* hat, mittens on left snowman and earmuff band; *red:* earmuffs, buttons, hat ball and brim and right snowman's scarf; *green:* scarf on left snowman and mitten on right snowman; *midnight:* sky; also shade snow and snowmen. Mix equal amounts of red and goldenrod; paint carrot noses with mixture. Add all outlines and embellishments with black.

4. Glue felt square to back of each tile.

5. Apply clear satin glaze to all painted surfaces. ❈

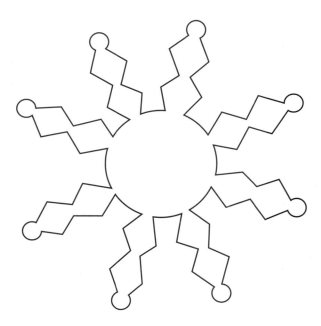

Snowflake Coaster

Patterns continued on page 152

Snowman Trivet

Precious Metals Plate

Transform a plain glass plate into an elegant display piece with any holiday rub-on transfer. Use the dish to dress up an ordinary shelf!

Design by Marlene Watson

Materials

- 12" glass or plastic serving platter
- Metallic silver partridge rub-on transfer*
- Wooden craft stick

Precious Metals Rub-On Art Transfer #PM307 from ChartPak.

Project Note

Refer to manufacturer's instructions for using rub-on transfer.

Instructions

1. Leaving tissue backing in place, cut off labeling at bottom of transfer sheet. Remove tissue and place transfer in center of plate.

2. Lift one corner of cover sheet slightly with index finger. Using craft stick, gently rub toward lifting finger, releasing top cover sheet. Repeat until cover sheet is released completely.

3. Leave transfer and plate undisturbed for at least 48 hours before washing; hand-washing is recommended. ❄

Snowy Lunch Box

*A basic lunch box painted with fanciful snowmen makes
a totally cool tote for your sandwich, your billfold or both!*

Design by Dorothy Egan

Materials

- New or used metal lunch box with domed lid
- All-purpose white primer*
- Satin finish*
- Acrylic paints*: lamp black, coral rose, true red, light buttermilk, milk chocolate, tangelo orange, navy blue
- Paintbrushes: ½", #2 and #4 shaders, 1" flat or foam brush, stiff bristle or old toothbrush
- White transfer paper
- Stylus

Primer and satin finish from Krylon; and Americana acrylic paints from DecoArt.

Project Notes

Refer to photo and patterns throughout.

Refer to directions for base-coating, rouging and shading under "Painting Techniques" in the General Instructions, page 190.

To transfer patterns, refer to instructions for "Using Transfer & Graphite Paper" in the General Instructions, page 190.

Let all coats of primer, paint and finish dry between applications.

Preparation

1. Wash and dry lunch box; set open lunch box in the sun to dry completely.

2. Spray lunch box inside and out with primer; base-coat with several coats navy blue.

Painting

1. Transfer pattern outlines to lunch box, positioning two snowmen on each side of lid, a plaid heart on center of box side, and another heart on each end of lid.

2. Apply three coats buttermilk to snowmen and one coat to hearts.

3. Transfer details to snowman as needed and paint:

Eyes, mouths and buttons: Dot on with black using tip of paintbrush handle or stylus; add short straight eyebrows with black and small brush. Highlight eyes with tiny buttermilk dots.

Cheeks: Rouge with coral rose; highlight with tiny buttermilk dots.

Nose: Paint orange; shade bottom edge with brown.

Scarf: Paint red; add buttermilk stripes; outline with black.

Outline: Outline snowmen with brown; outline again with fine line of black.

Arms: Add arms with brown.

4. Over-paint hearts with red. Add plaid lines with buttermilk.

5. Outline hearts with brown; using black, add primitive-style "stitches" over outline.

6. Lightly pencil lettering along bottom edges of lunch box. Sample has "Let's do Lunch!" on front, "A Hot Lunch on a snowy day" on back, "Hot Cocoa" on one end and "Warm Friends" on the other. Paint lettering with buttermilk; erase visible pencil lines.

7. Using stiff bristle brush or old toothbrush, spatter painted lunch box with buttermilk.

8. Spray lunch box with several coats of satin finish. ❄

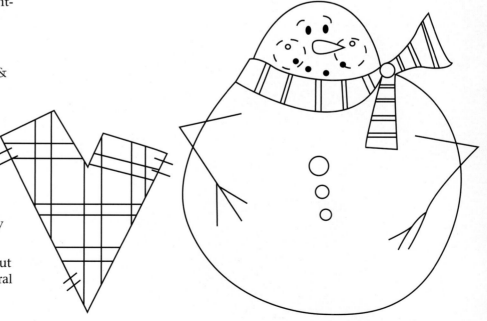

Plaid Heart   **Snowman**

Snowflake Washtub

Fill this decorative washtub with ice to keep your drinks cold during your next holiday party.

Design by Annie Lang

Materials

- 15½" x 10" x 5½" galvanized washtub
- Vinegar
- Graphite paper
- Metal paints*: bright white, cornflower blue, bright blue, bright silver
- Crystal glitter paint*
- Small sponge
- Foam brush
- Paintbrushes: #8 filbert, #0 and #2 pointed rounds
- 16 diamond-shape silver jewel gemstones
- Jewel glue*

No-Prep Metal Paints and Craft Twinkles glitter paint from DecoArt; and Gem-Tac adhesive from Beacon.

Project Notes

Refer to pattern and photo throughout.

To transfer pattern, refer to instructions for "Using Transfer & Graphite Paper" in the General Instructions, page 190.

Let all paints dry between applications.

Once adhesive has set in last step, tub is waterproof and ready for use.

Instructions

1. Wash tub inside and out with a mixture of equal parts water and vinegar to remove any oils or factory residue.

2. Wrap washtub handles with masking tape to protect finish from paint.

3. Using foam brush, base-coat exterior of tub—sides and bottom—with two coats cornflower blue.

4. Dampen sponge in water;

squeeze out excess until sponge is nearly dry. Dip sponge into bright blue paint and tap sponge up and down on palette a few times to evenly distribute paint. Apply paint over base-coated areas, gently pouncing sponge up and down, and allowing some of the cornflower blue to show through. Remove tape from handles when paint is dry.

5. Transfer pattern to sides of painted washtub, repeating pattern as needed so that evenly spaced snowflakes circle the washtub.

6. Using filbert brush, paint each snowflake white; add a second coat if needed.

7. Using white paint throughout, add pattern of dots around snowflakes with #0 round brush; using #2 round, add swirls between snowflakes.

8. Using #2 round brush and silver, outline snowflakes.

9. Using filbert brush, paint each snowflake with glitter paint.

10. Glue gemstone in center of each snowflake. ❄

Festive Fashions

Spread Christmas cheer wherever you go by wearing holiday garments throughout the Yuletide season! From colorful sweatshirts and vests to sparkling jewelry, you can deck yourself in a little or a lot of holiday cheer as you wish!

Little Cookie Sweatshirt

"Sugar and spice and everything nice"—that's what little gingerbread girls are made of!

Design by Chris Malone

Materials

- Child's red sweatshirt
- Fabrics: 7" x 8" ginger-color solid, scrap of pink with white pin dots
- 6-strand embroidery floss: red, black, white
- Embroidery needle
- White gathered eyelet lace: 2¼ yards 1¼"-wide, 2¾" 2¼"-wide
- Buttons: 2 (⅛") flat black, ¾" flat red heart
- Red grosgrain ribbon with white pin dots: 9" ⅜"-wide, 12" ⅝"-wide
- Iron-on adhesive*
- Pressing paper
- Fabric adhesive*
- Seam sealant
- Red sewing thread
- Sewing machine
- Iron

*HeatnBond Lite iron-on adhesive from Therm O Web; and Fabri-Tac adhesive from Beacon.

Project Notes

Refer to photo and patterns throughout.

Sweatshirt used for sample project is size 5. Use a photocopier with enlarging/reducing capabilities to enlarge or reduce pattern as needed for garments of different sizes.

Use 3 strands separated from 6-strand embroidery floss for all stitching unless otherwise instructed.

Follow manufacturer's instructions for using iron-on adhesive.

Instructions

1. Wash and dry sweatshirt without using fabric softener; iron to remove wrinkles.

2. *Appliqué:* Trace gingerbread girl and two cheeks onto paper side of iron-on adhesive. Cut out pieces ⅛" outside traced lines.

3. Iron gingerbread girl onto wrong side of ginger-color fabric; iron cheek circles onto pink pin-dot fabric. Cut out along traced lines.

4. Peel backing from fused pieces;

Continued on page 163

Gingerbread
Cut 1 from fused ginger fabric

Cut 2 cheeks from fused pink pin-dot

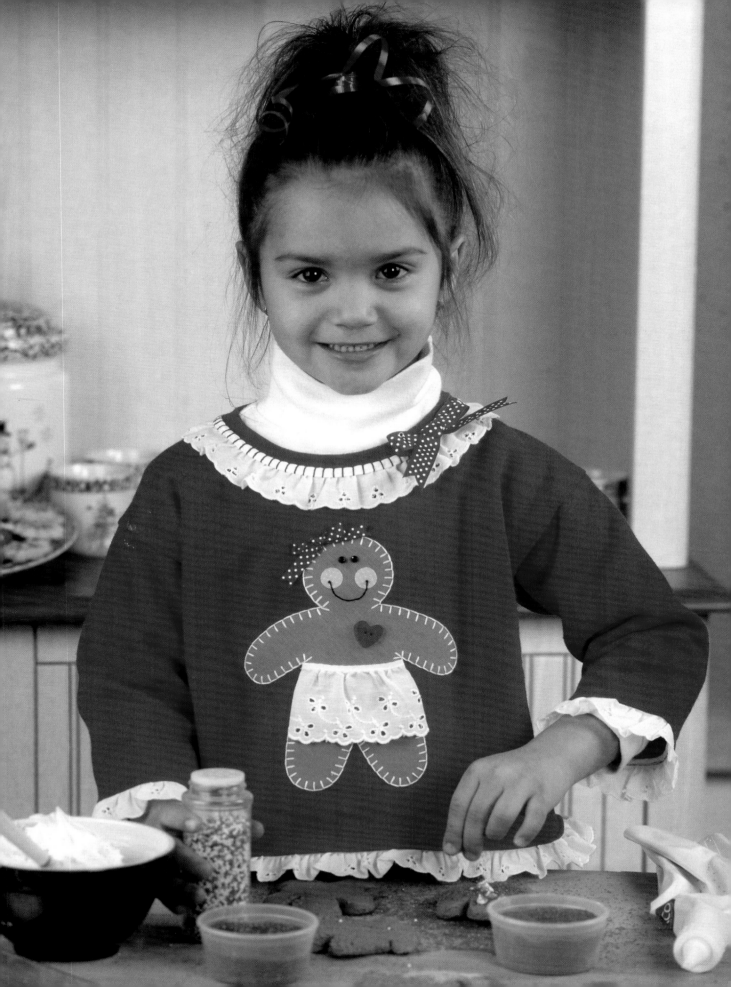

Candy Canes Necklace & Brooch

The rich colors of these fun-to-paint accessories are accented with simple woodburning.

Designs by Vicki Schreiner

Materials

Necklace & Brooch

- Wooden hearts (curved or flat)*: 2", 2½"
- Woodburning tool with mini flow point*
- Clear finish glaze base*
- Satin interior varnish*
- Brown antiquing gel*
- Acrylic paints*: tompte red, hunter green, white, opaque blue, eucalyptus
- Paintbrushes: #4 shader, #3 and #1 rounds
- 2 (3mm x 12mm) nickel screw eyes
- Round wooden beads: 4 (7⁄16") dark blue, 4 (½") red, 2 (5⁄8") green
- 1"–1½" pin back
- Jewelry findings: 4 jewelry and
- craft end caps with loop, 2 (3⁄16") jump rings, barrel clasp
- 1⅓ yards green satin rat-tail cord
- Tacky adhesive*
- Needle-nose pliers
- Graphite paper
- Fine sandpaper
- Ballpoint pen
- Paper towels
- Transparent tape
- Toothpick
- Stylus or brush handle

Wooden hearts from Viking Woodcrafts; Creative Woodburner #5567 with Mini Flow Point #5593 from Walnut Hollow; Ceramcoat clear Faux Finish Glaze Base, satin interior varnish, Antiquing Gel and acrylic paints from Delta; and Ultimate Tacky Adhesive from Crafter's Pick.

Project Notes

Refer to photo and pattern throughout. Pattern shown is for pin (2" heart); use a photocopier with enlarging capabilities to enlarge pattern 128 percent before transferring it to 2½" heart for necklace.

See directions for transferring pattern under "Using Transfer & Graphite Paper" in the General Instructions, page 190. Do not transfer stippling dots; these are for your reference when shading.

Follow manufacturer's instructions for using woodburning tool, heeding safety precautions. Change tip to mini flow point and tighten with needle-nose pliers.

Before woodburning project, practice on scrap wood. Hold tool like a

Candy Canes Jewelry
Transfer as shown for pin
Enlarge pattern 128% before
transferring for necklace

pen and use slow, short strokes to try straight and curved lines. Using a tapping motion, make clusters of stippled dots.

To maintain even heat flow, clean tool occasionally by dragging tip across sandpaper.

Mix paints with an equal amount of glaze base for steps 1–3 of Painting & Detailing. Use undiluted paints for holly berries and dots in step 5.

Use appropriate brush to fit area you are painting.

Let all paints, antiquing gel and varnish dry between applications.

Woodburning

1. Transfer design to 2" heart for brooch or enlarge design to 2½" heart for necklace.

2. Using mini flow point, wood-burn outlines; do not outline stripes on candy canes or holly berries. For shading, burn clusters of stippled dots on holly leaves.

Painting & Detailing

1. *Paint design: inner heart:* blue; *border stripe:* red; *outer border, sides and back of heart:* hunter green; *wide stripes on candy canes:* alternating white and red; *holly leaves:* eucalyptus.

2. Using #1 round brush, line thin red stripes onto wide white stripes.

3. Shade holly leaves by dabbing on a very tiny amount of hunter green and patting the applied paint with brush to blend and soften.

4. Apply one coat antiquing gel to all surfaces; wipe off with paper towel. Let dry.

5. Dot on holly berries using stylus or brush handle dipped in red; let dry, then use toothpick dipped in

white to add tiny highlight dot to each berry. Let dry.

6. Apply three coats of varnish to entire heart, drying between coats.

Finishing Brooch

Glue pin back to back of painted 2" heart.

Finishing Necklace

1. Position screw eye in each side of heart 2¼" up from bottom point.

2. Cut rat-tail cord in half; string each length through a screw eye.

3. Wrap ends of one cord as tightly as possible with transparent tape; cut taped ends on an angle to form point.

4. String beads on cord in order: blue, red, green, red, blue. **Note:** *If holes in beads are too small, enlarge them with craft drill using ⅛" bit.*

5. After stringing beads, measure cord out from screw eye and cut to 11" long. Using needle-nose pliers, add an end cap, then a jump ring.

6. Repeat steps 3–5 on second cord.

7. Attach barrel clasp halves to jump rings on ends of cords. ❀

Little Cookie Sweatshirt

Continued from page 160

position gingerbread girl on front of sweatshirt 2½" down from neck edge. Place cheeks on face. Using pressing paper, fuse pieces to shirt.

5. Blanket-stitch around gingerbread girl with white floss. Draw smile on her head and backstitch with black floss, adding a French knot at each end of smile. Using black floss, sew black buttons to face for eyes.

6. *Bottom and sleeve edges:* Cut off ribbing at bottom of shirt. Cut ribbing cuffs *plus* 1¾" off each sleeve. Cut three pieces of 1¼"-wide eyelet lace long enough to fit around

bottom of shirt *plus* 1"; cut two more pieces long enough to fit around cut edges of sleeves *plus* 1". Treat ends with seam sealant; let dry.

7. Starting at one side of bottom, machine-stitch bound edge of lace to bottom of sweatshirt, right sides facing, using red thread. Sew all around, overlapping ends ½"; trim if necessary. Turn edge of sweatshirt in to wrong side; by machine, top-stitch through shirt and lace ⅛" from fold. Repeat procedure to attach lace trim to sleeves, beginning and ending at underarm seams.

8. *Neck edge:* Cut a piece of 1¼"-wide eyelet lace long enough to fit around neck of sweatshirt at base of ribbing *plus* 1". Apply seam

sealant to cut ends; let dry.

9. Starting at center back, blanket-stitch lace at base of ribbing with 4 strands red floss, making stitches long enough to cover finished edge of lace trim. To finish, fold under raw end and overlap beginning end ½".

10. *Finishing:* Apply seam sealant to cut ends of 2¼" eyelet lace; let dry. Glue top edge of lace across gingerbread girl for apron. Sew heart button in place.

11. Tie each piece of ribbon into a bow; cut notches in ends and treat with seam sealant; let dry. Glue or tack smaller bow to gingerbread girl's head off to left side, and larger bow to sweatshirt at neckline off to right side. ❀

Button Fun Sweatshirts

Here are three fun projects for using up that stash of odd buttons and remnants of ribbon! They're a great project for crafting with the kids!

Designs by Bev Shenefield

Woven Ribbon Tree Shirt

Materials

- Women's large red sweatshirt
- Assorted green ribbons
- Buttons: 1" gold star shank*, large shank for base, various small assorted
- Fusible web
- Jewel glue*
- Macramé board
- Straight pins
- Wire cutters or craft snips
- Iron

Star shank button from JHB Buttons; and Jewel Bond Glue from Crafter's Pick.

Project Notes

Refer to photo throughout.

Wire-edge ribbons can be used if wire is removed.

Refer to manufacturer's instructions for using fusible web.

Instructions

1. Wash and dry sweatshirt without using fabric softener to remove sizing.

2. Cut ribbons into 12" pieces.

3. Pin ribbons lengthwise and side by side to macramé board, starting in center and pinning ends of ribbons to hold them in place. If ribbons have a wrong side, make sure wrong side faces up.

4. Weave remaining ribbons under and over lengthwise ribbons, again making sure wrong side faces up.

5. Lay fusible web over ribbons, rough side down. Fuse to woven ribbons. When cool, cut into a triangular tree shape 9¾" tall and 10" across at base, leaving center vertical ribbon full length at bottom for tree trunk; trim trunk so that it extends 1½"–2" below tree.

6. Remove paper backing; fuse tree to center front of shirt.

7. Snap shanks off all buttons using wire cutters or craft snips. Glue assorted small buttons over tree for ornaments; glue star button at top of tree; glue large button at bottom of ribbon tree trunk. Let glue cure for 24 hours before wearing.

Button Tree Shirts
Materials

- 2 white sweatshirts in desired sizes
- Buttons: 1" gold star shank*, yellow stars (optional), green triangular, various assorted (see Project Notes)
- Jewel glue*
- Wire cutters or craft snips

*Star shank button from JHB Buttons; and Jewel Bond Glue from Crafter's Pick.

Project Notes

Refer to photo throughout.

On sample adult-size shirt, tree is made up mostly of assorted green buttons in flat and shank styles, interspersed with yellow star buttons. Tip of tree is a 1⅛" green triangular button; base of tree is formed by a ¾" green triangular button positioned with point down between two ¾" gold-tone octagonal buttons.

On sample child-size shirt, tree is made up of shank buttons in assorted colors. Tip of tree is a ¾" green triangular button; base of

tree is a ¾" red square button.

Instructions

1. Wash and dry sweatshirts without using fabric softener to remove sizing.

2. Snap any shanks off buttons using wire cutters or craft snips. Glue buttons to front of shirt in a tree pattern. On sample adult shirt, body of tree measures 8½" wide x 7" tall, excluding star at top, trunk and base. On sample child shirt, body of tree measures 6" wide x 4½" tall, excluding base. Vary size of tree as desired to fit your shirt. Let glue cure for 24 hours before wearing. ❊

Button Bouquet Gloves

Enhance inexpensive knit gloves with bouquets of bright button flowers and green ribbon leaves for a great holiday gift!

Design by Chris Malone

Materials

- Black stretch knit gloves
- ⅞"–1" buttons: 2 each bright yellow, bright red, bright blue
- Ribbon: 12" ⅞"-wide green satin, 18" ⅜"-wide black-and-white checked
- Sewing thread: black, green
- Hand-sewing needle
- Adhesive*
- Cardboard to fit inside glove

Fabri-Tac adhesive from Beacon.

Project Note

Refer to photo and Figs. 1 and 2 throughout.

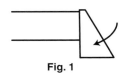

Fig. 1

Fig. 2

Instructions

1. Slide cardboard into glove to keep from sewing both sides together. Using black thread, sew one button of each color to glove, overlapping buttons slightly.

2. *Leaves:* Cut green ribbon into six 2" pieces. Fold ends of one piece down toward center (Fig. 1). With green thread, sew gathering stitch across bottom edge (Fig. 2) and pull thread to gather tightly. Wrap thread ends around stitches; knot and clip thread ends. Trim excess ribbon to within ¼" of stitching. Repeat with remaining green ribbon to make six leaves. Apply adhesive to stem end of each leaf; tuck under buttons.

3. Cut checked ribbon into two 9" pieces. Tie each in a bow. Glue one bow off to one side of button arrangement on each glove (or tack it in place with a few stitches). Notch ends of bow streamers. ❄

Santa's Little Helper Sweatshirt

Paint this enthusiastic holiday elf on a sweatshirt—or a bib apron!—for your little helper.

Design by Annie Lang

Materials

- White sweatshirt (see Project Notes)
- Tracing paper
- Fabric transfer pen or pencil
- Fabric acrylic paints*: white, calico red, peaches and cream, true blue, baby blue, bright green, kelly green, black
- Clear glimmer metallic glitter fabric paint*
- Fabric acrylic fluorescent paints* (optional): fiery red, thermal green
- Paintbrushes: #16, #8, #4 and #2 flat scrubbers, #4 and #2 round scrubbers, #1 liner
- Shirt-painting board or heavy cardboard cut to fit inside sweatshirt and covered with large plastic bag
- Iron

So-Soft and Heavy Metals Liquid Glitter fabric paints from DecoArt; and Hot Shots fluorescent fabric paint.

Project Notes

Sample is a child's size 6–8 sweatshirt.

Refer to photo and pattern throughout.

Enlarge pattern 110 percent before transferring to shirt.

To transfer patterns, refer to instructions for "Using Transfer & Graphite Paper" in the General Instructions, page 190.

This project is "coloring book" painted: Simply fill in areas with paint as directed, as if you were coloring the pages of a coloring book.

Refer to directions for base-coating under "Painting Techniques" in the General Instructions, page 190.

Shading: Load one side of flat brush with shading color, then sweep brush back and forth on palette a few times to work paint into brush. *While base-coat color is still wet,* apply shading around edges of area you are working on and then gently blend colors together.

Preparation

1. Wash sweatshirt without using fabric softener to remove sizing. Dry on cool setting or line dry.

2. Transfer design to front of sweatshirt.

Painting

1. *Add background shadowing to make design appear more dimensional:* Dampen area to be painted with water. *Do not* thin paint with water. Follow right side border edges of motif with baby blue so shadows will appear on right. Apply additional shadowing just below bottom edge of banner. Let dry.

2. *Face and hands:* Using #4 round brush, paint face, tongue and hands with peach. Combine a bit of calico red with peach. Using #4 flat brush, float this shading color around edges of face, along left side of fingers, and to fill in inner ears; using #4 round, tap shading color onto cheeks. Use #2 round to add calico red nose. Mix a tiny bit of black into some calico red; while still wet, apply this shading color to underside of nose. When dry, use liner to add tiny white highlight dots to cheeks, nose and tops of fingers.

3. *Hair, eyes and mouth:* Using #2 round brush, paint hair strands with white; fill in inner mouth with black using #4 round. Using #1 liner and black, paint eyes.

4. *Bow tie and hat:* Paint pompom on tip of hat white. While still wet, swirl some baby blue around edges to make it appear "fluffy." Base-coat hat and bow areas with calico red using #16 flat brush. Mix a tiny bit of black into some calico red; while areas are still wet, apply this shading color to border edges with #8 flat brush. If desired, add dramatic highlights by applying fiery red to upper right border edges of hat, down each section of bow and then onto the center knot of bow.

5. *Banner:* Base-coat with baby blue using #16 flat brush. Using #8 brush, shade fold areas and edges with true blue. When dry, use #1 liner to add black lettering.

6. *Candy cane frame:* Using #2 flat brush, paint every other stripe calico red. Mix a tiny bit of black into calico red; while red stripes are still wet, apply a touch of this shading color to right side of candy canes and around all holly leaf border edges where they overlap onto stripes. Repeat for white stripes, base-coating each with white and then shading with baby blue. When dry, apply white highlight line across stripes using #1 liner. Top cane is highlighted near upper edge and side canes are highlighted near left edges.

7. *Holly and berries:* Use #4 round brush to paint berries calico red. When dry, use liner to add tiny white highlight dot to each. Using #4 and #2 flat brushes, paint right section of each leaf kelly green and left section with bright green. If desired, add dramatic highlights by substituting *thermal green for bright green* on each leaf.

8. *Outlining and details:* Using liner and black, paint all outlining and detail lines.

9. When paint is completely dry, brush over candy canes and banner with clear glimmer. ❈

Santa's Little Helper
Enlarge 110% before transferring

Reindeer Hat

This warm cap is perfect for all kinds of reindeer games—at Christmastime and all winter long!

Design by Angie Wilhite

Materials

- Purchased taupe knit hat
- Felt*: 3" x 6" piece white, 4" x 6" piece heather, ¼ yard brown, 4" square black
- ¼ yard iron-on adhesive*
- ¼ yard pressing paper*
- Fusible products*: 6" square fusible interfacing, ⅛ yard fusible fleece
- Embroidery floss*: black #310, dark beige gray #642, black brown #3371
- 1" red pompom
- Needle
- Fabric adhesive*
- Iron

Felt from CPE; HeatnBond Lite iron-on adhesive and pressing paper from Therm O Web; Sof-Shape fusible interfacing and Fusible Fleece from Pellon; and DMC embroidery floss.

Project Notes

Refer to photo and patterns throughout.

Follow manufacturers' instructions for using fusible products.

Instructions

1. Wash hat without using fabric softener; dry.

2. Apply fusible interfacing to back of white felt. Apply fusible adhesive to backs of white and black felt. Cut two eyes from white felt; remove paper backing. Position eyes on hat cuff and fuse in place. Cut pupils from black felt; fuse over eyes.

3. Using 2 strands black embroidery floss, blanket-stitch around eyes and pupils. Glue pompom to cuff for nose.

4. Cut heather felt into four 3" squares; cut brown felt into four 4" x 6" pieces. Apply fusible adhesive to two pieces each of heather and brown felt. Remove paper backing; apply fusible fleece to other pieces of heather and brown felt. Position matching felt pieces wrong sides together and fuse.

5. Cut two ears, reversing one, from fused heather felt and two antlers, reversing one, from fused brown felt. Using 2 strands brown embroidery floss, blanket-stitch around ears. Using 2 strands gray floss, blanket-stitch around antlers.

6. Glue ears to antlers. Glue antlers inside hat cuff. ❄

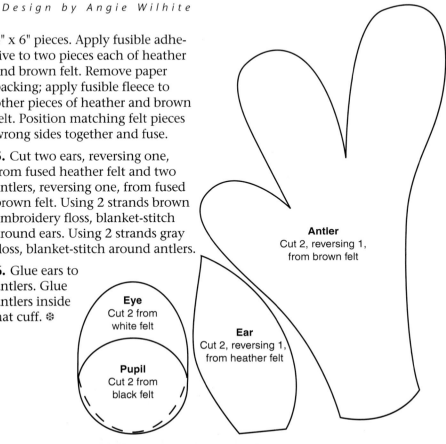

Antler
Cut 2, reversing 1, from brown felt

Eye
Cut 2 from white felt

Pupil
Cut 2 from black felt

Ear
Cut 2, reversing 1, from heather felt

Snowmen Slippers

Adorn ready-made slip-ons with frosty snowmen to keep toes toasty warm on winter mornings!

Design by Vicki Schreiner

Materials

- House slippers*
- ¼ yard red plaid flannel
- 2 (7½") pieces ⅜"-wide hunter green decorative braid
- Shank buttons: 2 (⁷⁄₁₆") round red, 4 (⅛") round black (or 6/0 black beads)
- Pink inkpad
- Felt*: black, 4" x 3" pieces each plush antique white and plush hunter green
- Fabric adhesive*
- 6-strand embroidery floss: black, red
- Sewing thread: red, hunter green
- Sewing and embroidery needles

House slippers from BagWorks; felt from Kunin; and Fabri-Tac adhesive from Beacon.

Project Note

Refer to photo, patterns and Slipper Assembly diagram throughout.

Instructions

1. *Cut fabric:* Cut two slipper tops from red plaid flannel. Cut two hat brims and face backings and two tops of hat from black felt. Cut two faces from antique white felt. Cut one of each scarf piece from green felt for left slipper; reverse pattern and cut one of each for right slipper. Cut two patches from green felt.

2. Using needle and thread, sew a gathering stitch along toe of each flannel piece as indicated by dashed lines on pattern.

3. Fold under edges of one piece of flannel to wrong side all the way around approximately ½" from edge to fit over actual slipper top up to seam; slightly gather the stitching to fit curved toe area of slipper; hold felt in place along seam with pins.

4. Center one piece of braid along top opening edge, pinning in place. Tuck ends of braid under flannel so that braid ends are between flannel and actual slipper; pin.

5. On outside of slipper, stitch flannel to slipper top along seam using tiny whipstitches with needle and matching thread; stitch braid to slipper using small whipstitches and stitching through all thicknesses of fabric.

6. Repeat steps 3–5 for second slipper.

Felt Snowmen

1. Using generous amounts of adhesive, glue face to fit onto hat brim. Glue top of hat to overlap behind brim; glue patch to top of hat along brim.

2. Stitch red button to center of face for nose; stitch black buttons in place for eyes. Using 3 strands black floss add straight-stitch eyebrows and backstitch mouth. Stitch patch onto hat using 3 strands red floss.

3. Rub your fingertip onto inkpad and apply blush to snowman's cheeks.

4. Glue snowman to flannel slipper top below braid; glue scarf bottom below face; glue scarf top onto scarf bottom. ❈

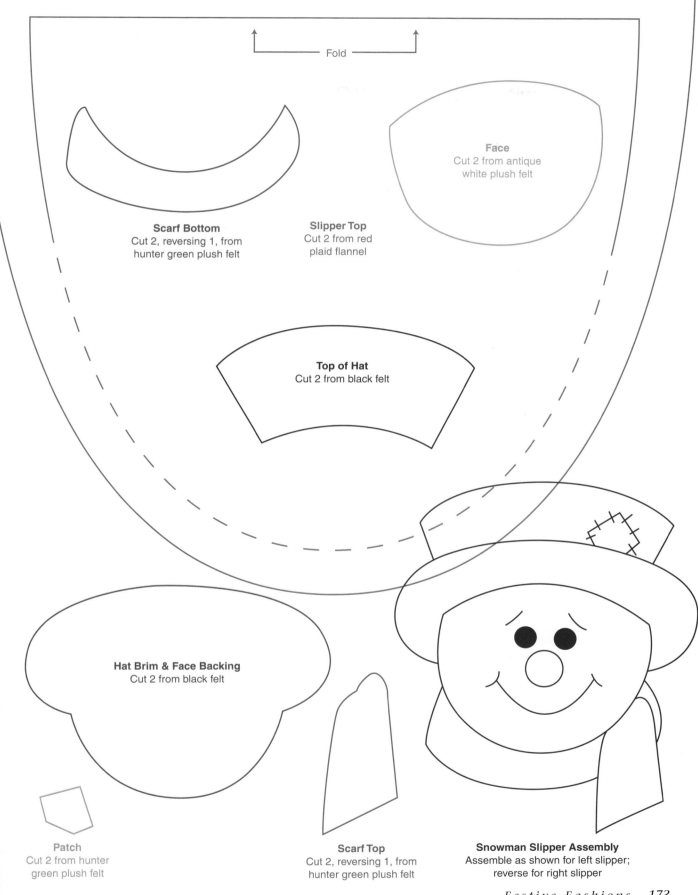

Fold

Scarf Bottom
Cut 2, reversing 1, from
hunter green plush felt

Slipper Top
Cut 2 from red
plaid flannel

Face
Cut 2 from antique
white plush felt

Top of Hat
Cut 2 from black felt

Hat Brim & Face Backing
Cut 2 from black felt

Patch
Cut 2 from hunter
green plush felt

Scarf Top
Cut 2, reversing 1, from
hunter green plush felt

Snowman Slipper Assembly
Assemble as shown for left slipper;
reverse for right slipper

Little Angel Jumper

Grandma doesn't need a reminder, but Santa might—
let everyone know your sweetie has been a good girl
by decking her out in this easy decorated jumper.

Design by Chris Malone

Materials

- Toddler's denim jumper (see Project Notes)
- Fabric scraps: dark rose, white-on-tan or white-on-ecru print, pale pink solid
- ⅜" gold plastic star button
- 14" ⅛"-wide dark rose satin ribbon
- 6-strand embroidery floss: black, white, pale pink to match pink fabric, medium brown, gold to match button
- Dark rose sewing thread
- Iron-on adhesive*
- Seam sealant
- Embroidery needle
- Air-soluble fabric marking pen
- Tissue paper (optional)
- Iron

HeatnBond Lite iron-on adhesive from Therm O Web.

Project Notes

Refer to photo and patterns throughout.

Denim jumper used for sample project is size 2T. Use a photocopier with enlarging/reducing capabilities to enlarge or reduce pattern as needed for garments of different sizes.

Use 2 strands separated from 6-strand embroidery floss for all blanket stitches and cross stitches. Use 4 strands for hair (lazy daisy stitches and French knots) and backstitching.

Follow manufacturer's instructions for using iron-on adhesive.

Instructions

1. Wash and dry jumper without using fabric softener; iron to remove wrinkles.

2. Trace three wings and three dresses onto paper side of iron-on adhesive, reversing one of each; trace three heads and three legs. Cut out pieces ⅛" outside traced lines.

3. Iron wings onto wrong side of white-on-tan print; iron legs and heads onto wrong side of pale pink solid; iron dresses onto wrong side of rose fabric. Cut out along traced lines.

4. Arrange two angels facing each other on skirt on front of jumper; arrange third angel on back bib of jumper. Remove paper backing; fuse legs and wings in place, then dresses, then heads.

5. Blanket-stitch around appliqués with embroidery floss using white along curved edges of wings, pale pink around heads and along curved edges of legs, and black along all exposed edges of dress. Re-press appliqués with iron as needed.

6. Using black floss, cross-stitch two eyes on each head where indicated by X's on pattern. For hair, use medium brown floss to stitch seven lazy daisy stitches radiating from top center of each head and add a French knot in center of lazy daisy stitches. Use air-soluble pen to mark halos over angels, referring to dashed lines on pattern; backstitch halos with gold floss.

7. Cut ribbon into three 8" pieces. Tie each in a ¾"–⅞" bow with ¾"–⅞" streamers; trim ribbon ends at an

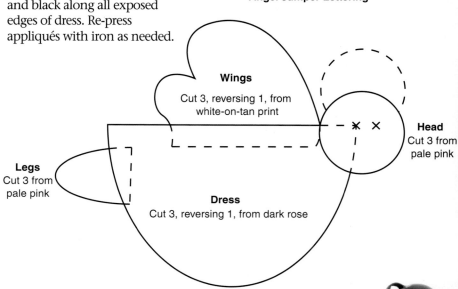

I've been an Angel

Angel Jumper Lettering

Wings
Cut 3, reversing 1, from white-on-tan print

Head
Cut 3 from pale pink

Legs
Cut 3 from pale pink

Dress
Cut 3, reversing 1, from dark rose

Angel Jumper

angle and treat with seam sealant. When dry, tack a bow at bottom of each angel's head with needle and rose sewing thread.

8. Transfer lettering onto front bib pocket with air-soluble marker. Backstitch lettering with gold floss, taking care not to stitch pocket closed. *Or,* trace lettering onto tissue paper; pin or tape paper in place. Backstitch through paper and fabric, then carefully tear away tissue paper.

9. Using gold floss, sew button to top left corner of pocket. ❁

Tree-Trimming Reindeer Vest

All decked out in tree lights and jingle bells, Rudolph is ready
to join your tree-trimming party on a colorful felt vest.

Design by Bev Shenefield

Materials

- Favorite vest pattern (see Project Notes)
- Felt*: 2 yards pirate green, 9" x 12" sheets red, gold, antique white, apple green, royal blue, coffee
- Sewing machine
- Green sewing thread to match pirate green felt
- Jewel glue*
- Iron-on adhesive backing
- Embroidery needles: regular and large-eye
- 2 (⅞") brown shank buttons
- 6-strand embroidery floss in colors to match each felt color, plus gray
- Fabric acrylic paints*: white, cadmium yellow, true blue, lamp black, Christmas green, soft red
- Paintbrushes: #20/0 liner, #2 filbert
- Iron
- Air-soluble marker or tailor's chalk
- Wire cutters or craft snips

Felt from Kunin; Gem Bond Glue from Crafter's Pick; and So-Soft fabric paints from Delta.

Project Notes

Refer to photo and patterns throughout.

Sample project was made using McCalls vest pattern #9840, size L, view A.

Follow manufacturers' instructions for using iron-on adhesive and fabric paints.

Let all paints dry between applications.

Instructions

1. Fold edges of vest pattern under along large-size lines, eliminating curves on sides. Width of each pattern piece will be 12"; check fit on wearer before cutting. Turn up edge of pattern so length is 6" shorter. Cut vest back and fronts from pirate green felt.

2. Iron adhesive backing onto backs of felt sheets. Trace patterns onto paper backing as follows and cut out: *red:* nine tree lights, one collar and nose; *gold:* 11 tree lights and three jingle bells; *antique white:* two antlers, reversing one; *apple green:* nine tree lights; *royal blue:* 10 tree lights; *coffee:* head and two ears, reversing one.

3. Iron reindeer pieces and jingle bells to back of vest as shown.

4. Using liner brush and black, paint reindeer's mouth and eyebrows, and details on jingle bells. Highlight nose with a comma stroke of red across top.

5. Referring to photo, plan arrangement of cord for tree lights, entwining it in antlers and up and over shoulder seams as shown. Continue curving cord down both front pieces of vest, making sure cord ends line up at shoulder seams. Also plan placement of tree lights along cord. *Note: On sample projects, there are 20 assorted tree lights on back of vest, 11 down right front of vest and eight down left front of vest.*

6. Iron tree lights in place. Highlight each with a comma stroke of paint near upper edge, using a mixture of green and white paints for apple green lights, blue paint for royal blue lights, red paint for red lights and yellow paint for gold lights. Combine a little black and white paint to make gray; use filbert to color the socket end of each tree light with mixture; add "threads" to sockets with liner brush and black. Let dry.

7. Using 2 strands of matching embroidery floss, blanket-stitch around all felt pieces.

8. Using 6 strands yellow floss through step 9, stitch lettering below reindeer on vest back.

9. Following line for tree light cord sketched in step 5, stitch running stitches of random lengths with very short spaces between each; do not include a space between the last tree light and shoulder seam; this will be done after seams are sewn.

10. Using 6 strands red embroidery floss, spiral floss around each yellow stitch two or three times without stitching through vest; then take short stitch to fill space between yellow stitches. Continue down entire length of cord.

11. Sew seams as pattern instructions direct. Trim seams and any uneven edges; press seams open.

12. Continue stitching cord over shoulder seams.

13. Using 2 strands bright green embroidery floss, blanket-stitch all edges of green felt vest.

14. Snap shanks off buttons with wire cutters; glue buttons to reindeer for eyes. ❄

LIGHTIN' SANTA'S WAY

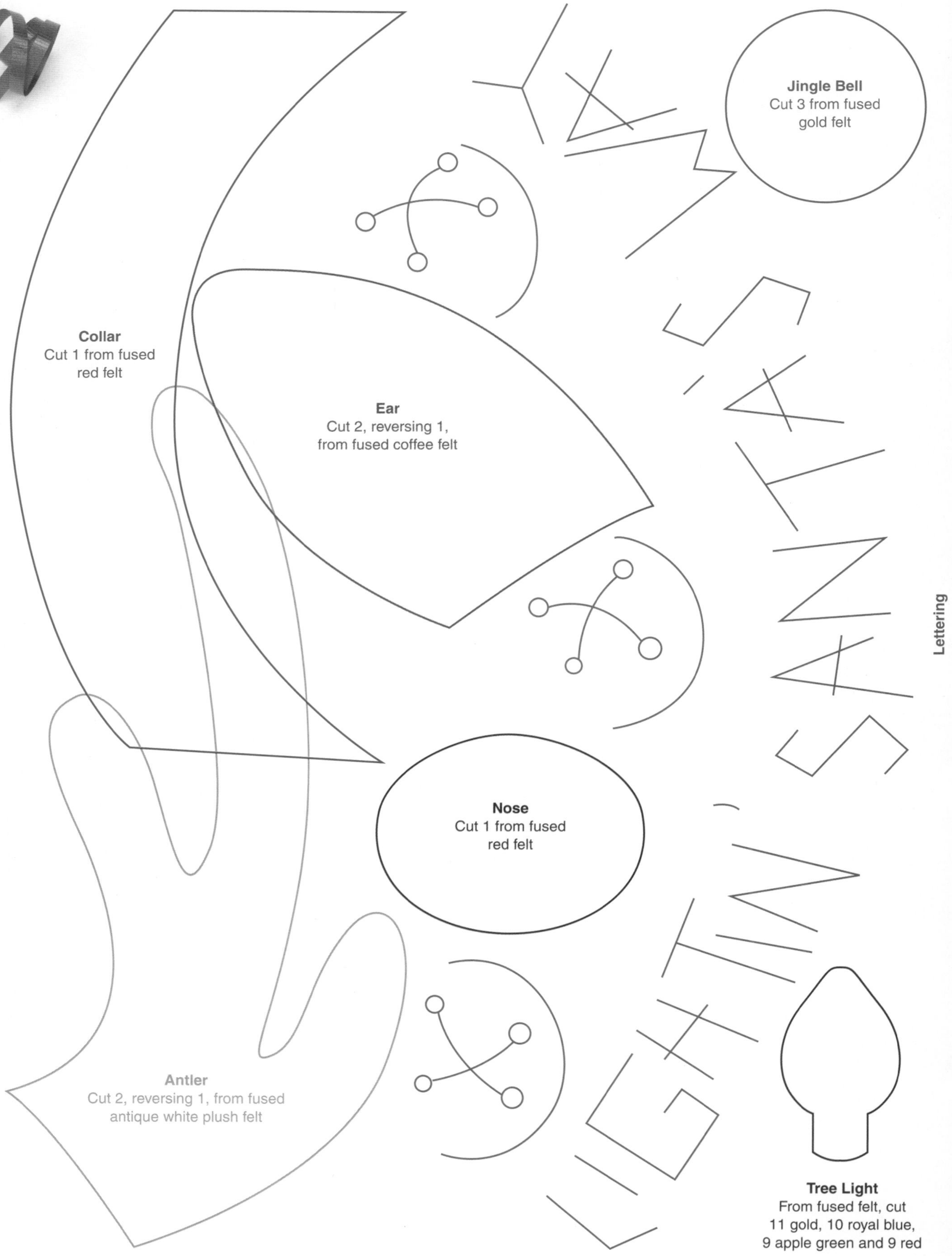

Jingle Bell
Cut 3 from fused
gold felt

Collar
Cut 1 from fused
red felt

Ear
Cut 2, reversing 1,
from fused coffee felt

LIGHTIN' SANTA

Lettering

Nose
Cut 1 from fused
red felt

Antler
Cut 2, reversing 1, from fused
antique white plush felt

Tree Light
From fused felt, cut
11 gold, 10 royal blue,
9 apple green and 9 red

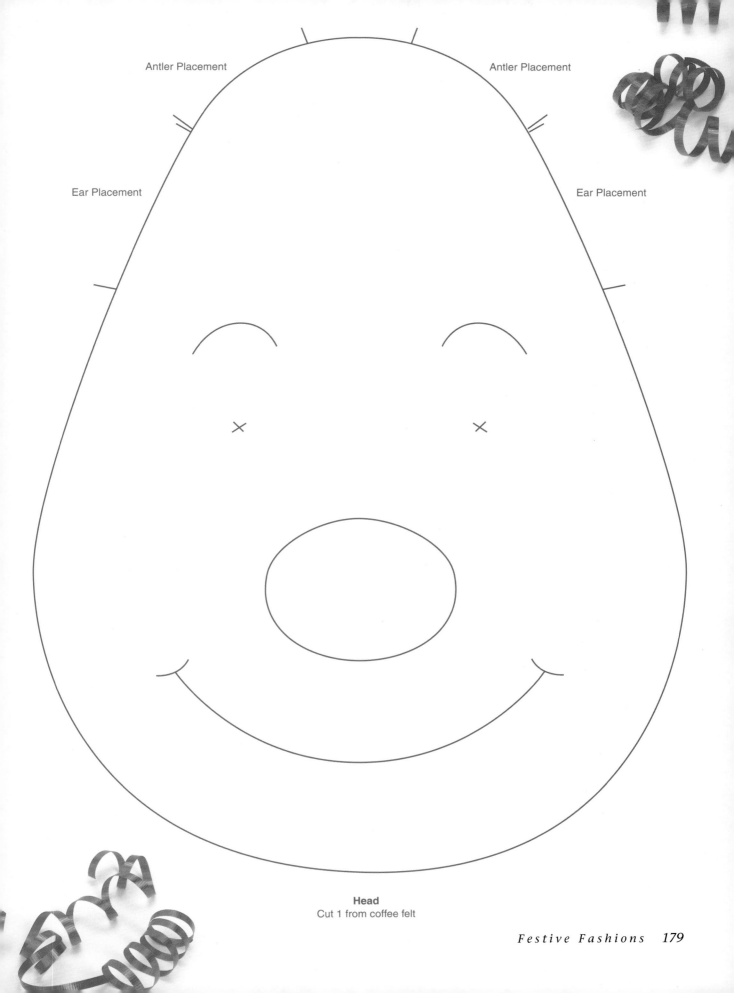

Antler Placement

Antler Placement

Ear Placement

Ear Placement

Head
Cut 1 from coffee felt

Paperclay Mitten Pins

Let your imagination run wild as you paint these fun pins in all sorts of fanciful patterns and designs!

Designs by Fran Farris

Materials

Set of 5 Pins

- 2 ounces modeling compound*
- Miniature mitten cookie cutter*
- Acrylic paints*: luscious lemon, ultra blue, pumpkin, GP purple, jubilee green, opaque red, pink parfait, Caribbean blue
- Paintbrushes: #8 shader, #10/0 spotter
- Large pieces cut from plastic garbage bags or plastic wrap
- Rolling pin
- Waxed paper or baking sheet, baking parchment and oven
- Emery board
- 5 (1") pin backs
- Craft cement

Creative Paperclay modeling compound and Ceramcoat acrylic paints from Delta.

Project Notes

Refer to photo throughout.

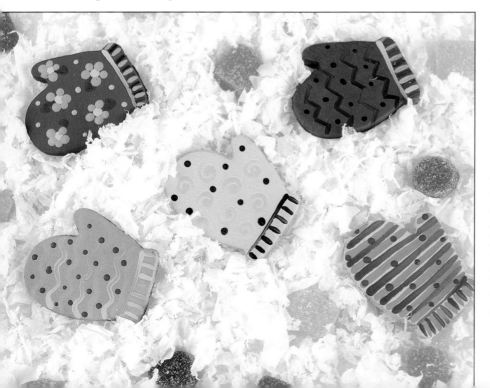

Follow manufacturer's instructions for working with Paperclay.

You may wish to keep a small container of water handy as you work for thinning and smoothing Paperclay.

Unless instructed otherwise, apply tiny dots of paint by dipping very tip of brush end of spotter brush in paint.

Instructions

1. Cover work surface with plastic. If work surface is waterproof, moisten it so plastic will stay in place.

2. Knead Paperclay to make it pliable, then roll it into a ball. Pat into a flattened disc. Lay Paperclay on one end of the plastic; fold other half of plastic over Paperclay and roll ¼" thick with rolling pin.

3. Using cookie cutter, cut five mittens. Lay shapes on waxed paper and let them air-dry, turning mittens over occasionally to prevent edges from curling.

Drying may take a few days depending on humidity. *Or,* place shapes on a baking sheet lined with baking parchment and bake in a preheated 250-degree oven for about 30 minutes or until dry; let cool completely.

4. Sand off any rough edges with emery board.

5. Using shader brush, paint all surfaces of mittens, painting one each with red, green, purple, Caribbean blue and yellow. Let dry.

6. Add painted details to mittens using spotter brush:

Opaque red mitten: Paint yellow line across top of cuff (at indentations in mitten). Fill cuff with alternating vertical stripes of pink and green. *Using pointed end of spotter brush handle dipped in paint,* dot yellow flower centers onto body of mitten and surround each with five pink petals. Using very tip of spotter brush's brush end, dot tiny pumpkin dots randomly between flowers. Paint tiny green stem and leaf on each flower.

Jubilee green mitten: Paint yellow line across top of cuff. Fill cuff with alternating vertical stripes of red and yellow. Paint four red zigzag lines horizontally across body of mitten. Dot tiny ultra blue dots onto green areas between red lines.

Purple mitten: Paint yellow line across top of cuff. Fill cuff with alternating vertical stripes of pink and yellow. Paint seven wavy lines horizontally across body of mitten, alternating pink and yellow. Dot tiny red dots onto purple areas between lines.

Caribbean blue mitten: Paint green

Heavenly Angel Barrette

Transform a button, ribbon and odds and ends into a beautiful barrette with celestial sparkle!

Design by Helen L. Rafson

Materials

- 1⅛" white 2-hole flat button
- Black fine-point permanent marking pen
- Acrylic paints: red, black
- Paintbrush handle with small tip
- Auburn brown 13mm doll hair*
- Acrylic satin-finish spray
- Ribbon: 3" ⅛"-wide metallic gold, 18¾" 1"-wide white grosgrain, 6⅛" ⅛"-wide blue satin
- Tacky craft glue
- Fabric adhesive*
- 2½" barrette
- 5-point 6mm metallic gold sequin stars*
- Gold seed beads
- Beading needle
- Gold thread
- Seam sealant

Doll hair from Darice; Aleene's Super Fabric Textile Adhesive from Duncan; and sequin stars from Nicole.

Project Notes

Refer to photo throughout.

Use tacky craft glue unless instructed otherwise.

Let ink, paints, acrylic spray, seam sealant and glues dry between applications.

Instructions

1. Using marker, draw eyelashes radiating from tops of button holes; draw smile. Dip end of paintbrush handle into red paint and dot cheeks onto ends of smile. Coat button with satin-finish spray.

2. Glue hair over top edge of button face. Glue ends of gold ribbon to back of button to form halo.

3. Tie white ribbon in a 4¼"-wide bow. Notch ends of streamers and treat with seam sealant. Position button face over knot of bow; check position of eyes and set button aside. Using black paint, paint area of knot where eyes will be located.

4. *Using knotted gold thread, sew stars to bow:* Bring needle up from back to front; thread on star sequin, then gold seed bead; take needle back down through sequin and through ribbon. Repeat to add beaded star sequins randomly and evenly over surface of bow.

5. Glue angel face to knot on bow. Tie blue ribbon in a 1⅛" bow with 1¼" streamers; trim ribbon ends at an angle and treat with seam sealant. Glue blue bow to white bow just under button face.

6. Using fabric adhesive, glue ribbon angel to barrette. ❋

Paperclay Mitten Pins

line across top of cuff. Fill cuff with alternating vertical stripes of green and pumpkin. Fill body with horizontal stripes of pumpkin and green, allowing a little blue to show between lines. Let dry. Dot tiny red dots onto pumpkin lines.

Yellow mitten: Using spotter, paint ultra blue line across top of cuff. Fill cuff with alternating vertical stripes of ultra blue and Caribbean blue. Paint Caribbean blue swirls randomly over body of mitten; add tiny ultra blue dots between swirls.

7. Cement a pin back onto back of each mitten. ❋

Skiing Cardinal Sweatshirt

The brilliant red of a cardinal on sparkling snow is a favorite wintertime motif.
This warm and cuddly sweatshirt brings it to life with a whimsical touch.

Design by Angie Wilhite

Materials

- Adult's white sweatshirt
- Fabric scraps: red print, black and gold solids, brown prints, green prints, black prints or checks
- All-purpose sewing threads to match fabrics
- Rayon embroidery threads to match fabrics
- Gold 6-strand embroidery floss
- Embroidery needle
- Fusible products*: ½ yard fusible transfer web, ⅛ yard fusible fleece, ⅛ yard fusible interfacing
- ¾ yard stitch-and-tear fabric stabilizer*
- Sewing machine with satin stitch attachment
- Iron

Pellon fusible products and Stitch-n-Tear fabric stabilizer from Plaid.

Project Notes

Refer to photo and patterns throughout.

Follow manufacturer's instructions for using fusible products.

Instructions

1. Wash and dry sweatshirt and fabrics without using fabric softener; press as needed to remove wrinkles.

2. Fuse interfacing to backs of all light-colored appliqué fabrics. Apply fusible fleece to back of red fabric, then transfer web to wrong side of all fabrics, including red.

3. Trace shapes onto paper sides of fused fabrics: Trace two wings, one head and one body onto red; one beak onto gold; face onto black; hat and brim onto black print and/or check; two skis onto brown print; three tree trunks onto brown print and three trees onto green print. Cut out pieces.

4. Remove paper backing; arrange cardinal, skis, hat and trees on front of sweatshirt. Fuse in place with iron.

5. Pin or baste stabilizer inside sweatshirt to cover design area. Using colors to match fabrics, thread sewing machine with rayon thread in top and all-purpose thread in bobbin. Satin-stitch around all elements of design beginning with those that appear to be in back (bottom layer) of design and working your way to front. Remove fabric stabilizer; trim threads.

6. Using 2 strands gold floss, sew two French knots for cardinal's eyes. ❄

Tree
Cut 3 from fused green print fabric

Tree Trunk
Cut 3 from fused brown print fabric

Patterns continued on page 184

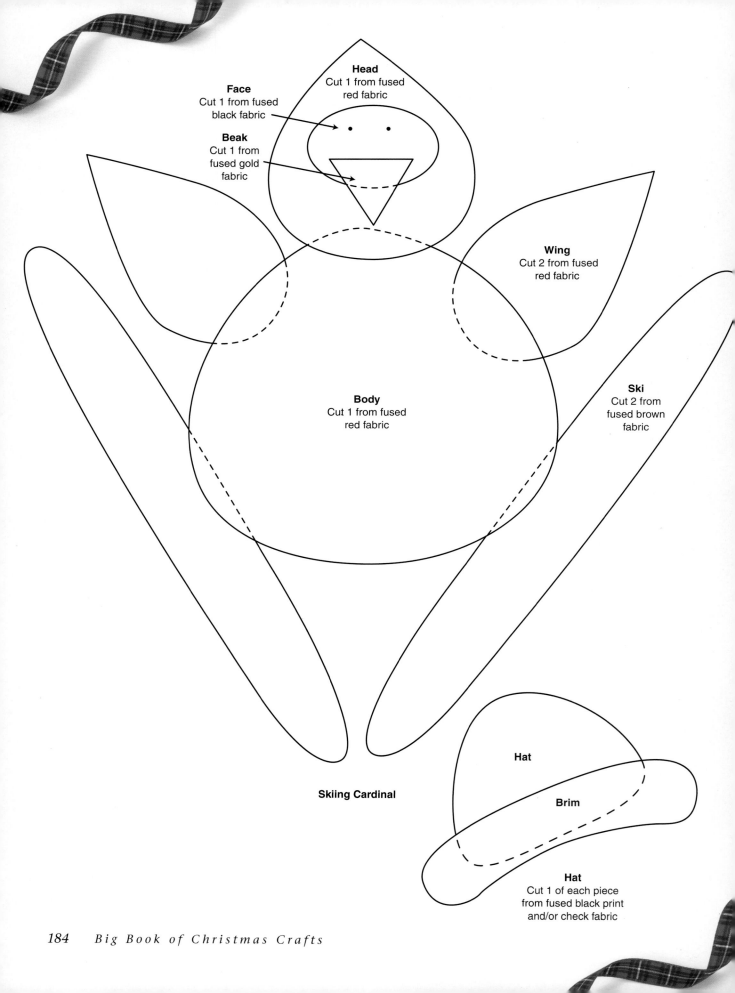

Head
Cut 1 from fused
red fabric

Face
Cut 1 from fused
black fabric

Beak
Cut 1 from
fused gold
fabric

Wing
Cut 2 from fused
red fabric

Body
Cut 1 from fused
red fabric

Ski
Cut 2 from
fused brown
fabric

Skiing Cardinal

Hat

Brim

Hat
Cut 1 of each piece
from fused black print
and/or check fabric

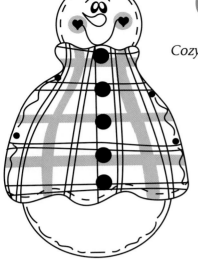

Caped Snowman Pin

Caped Snowman Pin

Cozy under his plaid wrap, this snowman has a warm, aged look thanks to simple shading and spattering effects.

Design by Mary Nelson

Materials

- Wooden snowman cutout* or ¼" pine or poplar stock at least 3" square
- Acrylic paints*: white wash, buttermilk, burnt orange, lamp black, mink tan, light avocado, teal green, black green, antique mauve, Napa red, soft blue
- Paintbrushes: ½" wash, ¼" angular shader, #2 shader, #0 and #6/0 liners
- Graphite paper
- Masking tape
- Cotton-tip swab
- Acrylic spray sealer
- Fine jute twine
- Craft cement
- 1¼" pin back
- Sandpaper (optional)
- Tack cloth (optional)
- Scroll saw (optional)

Wooden cutout from My Favorite Things and Americana acrylic paints from DecoArt.

Project Notes

Refer to photo and pattern throughout.

To transfer pattern, refer to instructions for "Using Transfer & Graphite Paper" in the General Instructions, page 190.

Painting: Use the largest brush that will fit the area to be painted. For line work, plaid lines and shading, thin paints with water to an inky consistency. Apply dots of paint with the end of paintbrush handle dipped in undiluted paint. Paint edges and back of snowman with adjacent colors used for base coat on front.

Let all paints and sealer dry between applications.

Instructions

1. If not using ready-made wooden cutout, cut pattern from wood with scroll saw. Sand edges and wipe off dust with tack cloth.

2. Cut a small piece of masking tape and press it onto back of snowman where pin back will be glued on later. Do not remove tape until painting is complete and sealer has been applied.

3. Transfer main pattern lines onto front of wood.

4. Paint head and body buttermilk; using cotton-tip swab, blush cheeks with mauve; shade with thinned tan. Add carrot nose with burnt orange; shade with thinned red.

5. Dot on eyes and mouth using undiluted black; line eyebrows and mouth with thinned black. Dot hearts onto ends of smile: Place two tiny dots of undiluted black next to each other and pull together at center bottom to form a heart. Add tiny white highlight dots to eyes.

6. Paint cape avocado. Add broad plaid lines with thinned blue; line on thin plaid lines with thinned teal. Shade cape with thinned black green; dot on buttons with undiluted black, and line on outline, center front line and simulated running stitch across bottom of cape with thinned black.

7. Spatter snowman lightly with thinned black.

8. Spray front, then back of snowman with sealer. Remove masking tape from back of snowman.

9. Holding two pieces of jute together, tie them in a single bow, trimming ends as necessary. Cement to front of snowman at neck.

10. Apply a generous amount of craft cement to back of snowman where pin back will be attached. Press pin back into cement, allowing cement to ooze through holes in pin back. Let pin set overnight before wearing. ❄

Mommy & Me Aprons

*Sweet memories are yours for the baking when you both
wear matching cover-ups sprinkled with painted treats.*

Designs by Vicki Schreiner

Materials
Both Aprons
- Adult's and child's white aprons*
- Textile medium*
- Clear finish glaze base*
- Acrylic paints*: burnt umber, burnt sienna, navy blue, tompte red, midnight blue, black green, Bridgeport grey, hunter green, black cherry, white, pink parfait
- Paintbrushes: #4 shader, #1, #3 and #6 rounds, #0 liner
- Black permanent fine-point pen*
- Black graphite paper
- 5 yards ⅜"-wide green satin ribbon with white pin dots
- Matching green thread and hand-sewing needle
- Sewing machine (optional)
- Masking tape
- Toothpick

Adult's #0182 and child's #0183 aprons from BagWorks; Ceramcoat Textile Medium, Clear Faux Finish Glaze Base and acrylic paints from Delta; and IdentiPen from Sakura.

Project Notes
Refer to photo and patterns throughout.

Patterns shown are for child's apron. Use a photocopier with enlarging capabilities to enlarge patterns 127 percent for adult's apron before transferring them to apron.

See directions for transferring patterns under "Using Transfer & Graphite Paper" in the General Instructions, page 190. Do not transfer stippling dots; these are for your reference when shading.

For base-coating and shading, mix paints with equal parts textile medium and glaze base.

For lining and dots, mix paints with equal part textile medium.

See directions for base-coating under "Painting Techniques" in the General Instructions, page 190.

Let all applications of paints and ink dry between coats.

Preparation
1. Wash aprons in cold water on gentle setting without using fabric softener. Dry on cool setting or line dry. Iron to remove all wrinkles.

2. Transfer gingerbread cookies to lower right area of aprons. Transfer outlines of peppermints to aprons, scattering them randomly from gingerbread across apron toward upper left.

Painting
1. *Base-coat areas using a single coat sufficient to cover fabric surface: all gingerbread heads, arms and feet:* burnt sienna; *collars, pants and heart buttons:* red; *child's bow and dress:* navy blue; *mommy's bow and dress:* hunter green; *peppermint stripes:* paint every other stripe red; it is not necessary to paint white areas on peppermints.

2. *Shade designs, working on small areas at a time:* For small areas use a #3 round brush; for larger areas, use #6 round brush. Load brush with a small amount of paint mixture, then dab or stroke onto areas to be shaded. Quickly stroke brush on paper towel to remove paint, then pat dry brush on applied paint to soften and blend. Allow to dry, then repeat as needed to darken. Shade as follows: *all gingerbread heads, arms and feet:* burnt umber; *collars, pants and heart buttons:* black cherry; *child's bow and dress:* midnight blue; *mommy's bow and dress:* black green; *red peppermint stripes:* black cherry; *white peppermint stripes and wrapper twists:* gray.

3. *Blush cheeks:* Using same technique as for shading, blush cheeks with pink.

4. *Lining:* Pull #0 liner through pool of paint, twirling as you go until bristles form a point. Use flowing strokes, making sure bristles are vertical, not on their sides. Use just the tip of the bristles, as you would a pencil. Line as follows: *child's collar:* navy blue; *mommy's collar:* hunter green; *gingerbread "frosting" lines:* white.

5. Using a toothpick dipped in white, apply dots to collars and a dot highlight to top right area of each heart button.

Finishing
1. Using fine tip of pen, outline designs. Do not outline stripes on peppermints or "frosting" lines on gingerbread. Fill in eyes and buttonholes on heart buttons.

2. Using a toothpick dipped in white, apply very tiny highlight dot to each eye.

3. By hand or machine, stitch ribbon onto outer binding of each apron. ✽

Peppermints
Reproduce as shown for child's apron
Enlarge patterns 127% before transferring
for Mommy's apron

Gingerbread Mommy & Child
Transfer as shown for child's apron
Enlarge 127% before transferring for
Mommy's apron

Buyer's Guide

Projects in this book were made using products provided by the manufacturers listed below. Look for the suggested products in your local craft- and art-supply stores. If unavailable, contact suppliers below. Some may be able to sell products directly to you; others may be able to refer you to retail sources.

Aleene's
Div. of Duncan Enterprises
5673 E. Shields Ave.
Fresno, CA 93727
(800) 237-2642
www.duncan-enterprises.com

Amaco
American Art Clay Co. Inc.
4717 W. 16th St.
Indianapolis, IN 46222-2598
(317) 244-6871
www.amaco.com

American Traditional Stencils/Stencil Outlet
442 First New Hampshire Turnpike
Northwood, NH 03261-9754
(800) 278-3624
www.American Traditional.com

Annie's Attic
1 Annie Ln.
Big Sandy, TX 75755
(800) 582-6643

API/The Adhesive Products Inc.
520 Cleveland Ave.
Albany, CA 94710
(510) 526-7616
www.crafterspick.com

Artist's Club
13118 N.E. Fourth St.
Vancouver, WA 98684
(800) 257-1077

Artistic Wire Ltd.
1210 Harrison Ave.
La Grange Park, IL 60526
(630) 530-7567
www.artisticwire.com

BagWorks Inc.
3301-C S. Cravens Rd.
Fort Worth, TX 76119
(800) 365-7423
www.bagworks.com

Beacon Adhesives/Signature Marketing
P.O. Box 427
Wyckoff, NJ 07481
(800) 865-7238
www.beacon1.com

The Beadery
P.O. Box 178
Hope Valley, RI 02832
(401) 539-2432

Bear With Us Inc.
3007 S. Kendall Ave.
Independence, MO 64055
(816) 373-3231

Bucilla Corp.
1 Oak Ridge Rd.
Humboldt Industrial Park
Hazleton, PA 18201-9764
(800) 233-3239

Charles Craft Inc.
P.O. Box 1049
Laurinburg, NC 28353
(910) 844-3521
e-mail: ccraft@carolina.net

ChartPak Rub-On Art
1 River Rd.
Leeds, MA 01053

Coats & Clark Consumer Service
P.O. Box 12229
Greenville, SC 29612-0229
(800) 648-1479
www.coatsandclark.com

CPE Inc.
P.O. Box 649
Union, SC 29379
(800) 327-0059

Crafter's Pick by API
520 Cleveland Ave.
Albany, CA 94710
(510) 526-7616
www.crafterspick.com

Crafter's Pride/Daniel Enterprises
P.O. Box 1105
Laurinburg, NC 28353
(910) 277-7441
www.crafterspride.com

Creative Paperclay Co. Inc.
79 Daily Dr., Suite 101
Camarillo, CA 93010
(805) 484-6648
www.paperclay.com

Darice Inc.
Mail-order source:
Bolek's
330 N. Tuscarawas Ave.
Dover, OH 44622
(330) 364-8878

DecoArt
P.O. Box 386
Stanford, KY 40484
(800) 367-3047
www.decoart.com

Delta Technical Coatings
2550 Pellissier Pl.
Whittier, CA 90601-1505
(800) 423-4135
www.deltacrafts.com

Design Works Inc.
170 Wilbur Pl.
Bohemia, NY 11716
(516) 244-5749

DMC Corp.
Hackensack Avenue, Bldg. 10A
South Kearny, NJ 07032-4688
(800) 275-4117
www.dmc-usa.com

Duncan Enterprises
5673 E. Shields Ave.
Fresno, CA 93727
(800) 237-2642
www.duncancrafts.com

Dow Flora Craft/Dow Chemical Co.
(800) 441-4369

Eclectic
995 S. A St.
Springfield, OR 97477
(800) 693-4667

EK Success Ltd.
125 Entin Rd.
Clifton, NJ 07014
(800) 524-1349
www.eksuccess.com

Fimo/Amaco
American Art Clay Co. Inc.
4717 W. 16th St.
Indianapolis, IN 46222-2598
(317) 244-6871
www.amaco.com

Fiskars Inc.
7811 W. Stewart Ave.
Wausau, WI 54401
(800) 950-0203, ext. 1277
www.fiskars.com

Forster Inc./Diamond Brands
1800 Cloquet
Cloquet, MN 55720
(218) 879-6700
www.diamondbrands.com/forster.html

Grafix Inc.
19499 Miles Rd.
Cleveland, OH 44128
(800) 447-2349
www.grafixarts.com

Innovo Inc.
1808 Cherry St.
Knoxville, TN 37917
(865) 546-1110

JHB International Inc.
1955 S. Quince St.
Denver, CO 80231
(303) 751-8100
www.buttons.com

Krylon/Sherwin-Williams Co.
Craft Customer Service
101 Prospect Ave. N.W.
Cleveland, OH 44115
(800) 247-3268
www.krylon.com

Kunin Felt Co./Foss Mfg. Co. Inc.
P.O. Box 5000
Hampton, NH 03842-5000
(603) 929-6100
www.kuninfelt.com

Lara's Crafts
590 N. Beach St.
Fort Worth, TX 76111
(800) 232-5272
www.larascrafts.com

Lion Brand Yarn Co.
34 W. 15th St.
New York, NY 10011
(800) 795-5466
www.lionbrand.com

The Little Fox Factory
931 Marion Rd.
Bucyrus, OH 44820
(419) 562-5420

My Favorite Things
P.O. Box 71
Dresden, NY 14441
(315) 536-6301
marycarl@eznet.net

Nicole Industries
P.O. Box 846
Mount Laurel, NJ 08054

Paper Reflections/DMD Industries Inc.
1250 ESI Dr.
Springdale, AR 72764
(800) 805-9890
www.dmdind.com

Pellon Consumer Products
3440 Industrial Dr.
Durham, NC 27704
(919) 620-3916

Plaid Enterprises Inc.
3225 Westech Dr.
Norcross, GA 30092
(800) 842-4197
www.plaidonline.com

Polyform Products Co.
1901 Estes Ave.
Elk Grove Village, IL 60007
(847) 427-0020
www.sculpey.com

Provo Craft
Mail-order source:
Creative Express
295 W. Center St.
Provo, UT 84601-4436
(800) 563-8679
www.creativeexpress.com

Royal Brush Mfg. Inc.
6707 Broadway
Merrillville, IN 46410
(219) 660-4170
www.royalbrush.com

Rubber Stampede Inc.
P.O. Box 246
Berkeley, CA 94701
(800) 632-8386
www.rstampede.com

Sakura Hobby Craft
2444 205th St., A-1
Torrance, CA 90501
(310) 212-7878
e-mail: craftman@earthlink.net

Sculpey III/Polyform Products Co.
1901 Estes Ave.
Elk Grove Village, IL 60007
(847) 427-0020
www.sculpey.com

Stampendous
1240 N. Red Gum
Anaheim, CA 92806-1820
(714) 688-0288
www.stampendous.com

St. Louis Trimmings
5040 Arsenal St.
St. Louis, MO 63139
(800) 325-7144

Syndicate Sales
P.O. Box 756
Kokomo, IN 46903
(765) 457-7277

Therm O Web
770 Glenn Ave.
Wheeling, IL 60090
(847) 520-5200
www.thermoweb.com

Toner Plastics
699 Silver St.
Agawam, MA 01001
(413) 789-1300
www.tonerplastics.com

Tsukineko
15411 N.E. 95th St.
Redmond, WA 98052
(800) 769-6633
www.tsukineko.com

Tulip
Div. of Duncan Enterprises
5673 E. Shields Ave.,
Fresno, CA 93727
(800) 237-2642
www.duncan-enterprises.com

Uniek
Mail-order source:
Annie's Attic Catalog
1 Annie Ln.
Big Sandy, TX 75755
(800) 582-6643

Viking Woodcrafts Inc.
1317 8th St. S.E.
Waseca, MN 56093
(800) 328-0116
www.vikingwoodcrafts.com

Walnut Hollow Farms Inc.
1409 St. Rd. 23
Dodgeville, WI 53533-2112
(800) 950-5101
www.walnuthollow.com

Warm & Natural/The Warm Co.
954 E. Union St.
Seattle, WA 98122
(800) 234-WARM
www.warmcompany.com

Weston Bowl Mill
Route 100
Weston, VT 05161
Chatsworth, CA 91311
(802) 824-6219

Yaley
7664 Avianca Dr.
Redding, CA 96002
(530) 365-5252
www.yaley.com

Zakware
Mail-order source:
Dishway
15 N. Brandon Dr.
Glendale Heights, IL 60139
(866) 347-4929
www.dishway.com

General Instructions

Materials

In addition to the materials listed for each craft, some of the following supplies may be needed to complete your projects. No doubt most of these are already on hand in your "treasure chest" of crafting aids. Gather them before you begin working so that you'll be able to complete each design quickly and without a hitch!

General Crafts

- Scissors
- Pencil
- Ruler
- Tracing paper
- Craft knife
- Heavy-duty craft cutters or wire nippers
- Plenty of newspapers to protect work surface

Painted Items

- Paper towels
- Paper or plastic foam plate or tray to use as a disposable paint palette for holding and mixing paints
- Plastic—a garbage bag, grocery sack, etc.—to protect your work surface
- Container of water or other recommended cleaning fluid for rinsing and cleaning brushes

Fabric Projects

- Iron and ironing board
- Pressing cloth
- Basic sewing notions
- Rotary cutter and self-healing mat
- Air-soluble markers
- Tailor's chalk

Reproducing Patterns & Templates

The patterns provided in this book are shown right side up, as they should look on the finished project; a few oversize patterns that need to be enlarged are clearly marked. Photocopiers with enlarging capabilities are readily available at copy stores and office supply stores. Simply copy the page, setting the photocopier to enlarge the pattern to the percentage indicated.

Patterns that do not need to be enlarged may be reproduced by placing a piece of tracing paper or vellum over the pattern in the book, and tracing the outlines carefully with a pencil or other marker.

Once you have copied your pattern pieces, cut them out and use these pieces as templates to trace around. Secure them as needed with pins or pattern weights.

If you plan to reuse the patterns or if the patterns are more intricate, with sharp points, etc., make sturdier templates by gluing the copied page of patterns onto heavy cardboard or template plastic. Let the glue dry, then cut out the pieces with a craft knife.

Depending on the application, it may be preferable to trace the patterns onto the wrong side of the fabric or other material so that no lines will be visible from the front.

In this case, make sure you place the right side of the pattern piece against the wrong side of the fabric, paper or other material so that the piece will face the right direction when it is cut out.

Using Transfer & Graphite Paper

Some projects recommend transferring patterns to wood or another material with transfer or graphite paper. Read the manufacturer's instructions before beginning.

Lay tracing paper over the printed pattern and trace it carefully. Then place transfer paper transfer side down on wood or other material to be marked. Lay traced pattern on top. Secure layers with low-tack masking tape or tacks to keep pattern and transfer paper from shifting while you work.

Using a stylus, pen or other implement, retrace the pattern lines using smooth, even pressure to transfer the design onto the surface.

Painted Designs

Disposable paper or plastic foam plates, including supermarket meat trays, make good palettes for pouring and mixing paints.

The success of a painted project often depends on the care taken in initial preparations, including sanding, applying primer and/or applying a base coat of color. Follow instructions carefully.

Take special care when painting adjacent sections with different colors; allow the first color to dry so that the second will not run or mix. When adding designs atop a painted base, let the base coat dry thoroughly first.

If you will be mixing media, such as drawing with marking pens on a painted surface, test the process and your materials on scraps to make sure there will be no running or bleeding.

Keep your work surface and your tools clean. Clean brushes promptly in the manner recommended by the paint manufacturer; many acrylics can be cleaned up with soap and water, while other paints may require a solvent. Suspend your paintbrushes by their handles to dry so that the fluid drains out completely and bristles remain straight and undamaged.

Work in a well-ventilated area when using paints, solvents or finishes that emit fumes; read product labels thoroughly to be aware of any potential hazards and precautions.

Painting Techniques

Base-coating: Load paintbrush evenly with color by dabbing it on palette, then coat surfaces with one or two smooth, solid coats of paint, letting paint dry between coats.

Comma strokes: Wet #1 script brush; dry on paper towel; dip into paint. Press tip of brush down so that bristles of brush spread out, then slowly pull brush toward you and up onto tip of brush; lift off.

Dry-brushing: Dip a dry round-bristle brush in paint; wipe excess paint off onto paper towel until brush is almost dry. Wipe brush across edges for subtle shading.

Floating: Dampen brush with water. Touch one side of brush to paint, then sweep brush back and forth on palette to work paint into the brush. Apply the color around the edges of the area you are working on as directed in painting instructions.

Rouging: Dip dry, round bristle brush in paint and wipe paint off onto paper towel until brush is almost completely dry and leaves no visible brush strokes. Wipe brush across area to be rouged using a circular motion.

Shading: Dip brush in water and blot lightly once on paper towel, leaving some water in brush. Dip point of brush into paint. Stroke onto palette once or twice to blend paint into water on bristles so that stroke has paint on one side gradually blending to no color on the other side. Apply to project as directed.

Side-loading and highlighting: Wet flat brush with water; dry on paper towel. Dip corner of brush into paint and brush back and forth on palette until color goes from dark value to light. Apply to project as directed.

Stenciling with brush: Dip dry stencil brush in paint. Wipe brush on paper towel, removing excess paint to prevent seepage under stencil. Brush cutout areas with a circular motion, holding brush perpendicular to surface. When shading, the brush should be almost dry, working only around edges. Use masking tape to hold stencil in place while working.

Stenciling with sponge: Use very little paint on the end of the sponge; too much paint applied at one time will cause the paint to seep under the edges of the stencil. Place a small puddle of paint on the palette, then dab a corner of the sponge into paint; blot off any excess onto palette, blending paint over surface of sponge. Using a light touch, dab sponge over stencil. When changing colors, rinse sponge thoroughly and wring out all traces of moisture. Any water left in sponge can cause paint to become more liquid and increase the possibility of paints seeping under stencil edges. ✸

Designer Index

Technique Index